Carving Wolves, Foxes and Coyotes

An Artistic Approach to Carving Canines in Wood

by

Desiree Hajny

FOX BOOKS
Fox Chapel Publishing Co Inc.

Fox Chapel Publishing Co., Inc.
1970 Broad Street
East Petersburg, PA 17520

Publisher: Alan Giagnocavo

Project Editor: Ayleen Stellhorn

Desktop Specialist: Linda L. Eberly

Reference Photography, Chapter 1:   Doug Lindstrand

Step-by-Step Photography: Mike Hutmacher

Cover Photography: Robert Polett

ISBN # 1-56523-098-1

To order your copy of this book,
please send check or money order
for $19.95 plus $2.50 shipping to:
Fox Books Orders
1970 Broad Street
East Petersburg, PA 17520

Manufactured in China

Dedication

This book is dedicated to two special people, Eldon and Judy Kline, my father and mother. In this day of searching for role models, they are, and have always been, heroes to me. Their patience, perseverance, love and support have inspired me through the years. Thank you for your friendship, as well as your love.

Table of Contents

Introduction

Change is good! Or at least that is what I think. The past year has seen some major changes in my life ranging from the direction my works have taken to my present location. After being away from home (Colorado) for twenty years, it feels good to get back to what I consider familiar surroundings. The canine book is something I've wanted to do for some time. There have been some that have accused me of not doing this title because I wasn't willing to share trade secrets. The truth of the matter is that I wasn't ready to undertake this project and feel that I could do it justice. My objective in writing books is to present a finished product that I feel is somewhat more advanced in scope and sequence than the previous rendering, and with improvements. This is the approach I have also attempted to pursue in my carving. I think some of the additions in this book will make this book a valuable resource for those interested in carving canines. Additions include many in the step-by-step section, plus in-depth expression charts, a greater inclusion of the young, and additional information on research that you will hopefully be able to apply to all aspects of your carving. As has been the case with all previous titles, this book should be considered an artistic approach to carving. I hope you are able to use it as a positive guide to improving your carving, but also utilize the skills and talents you possess that will make your works unique to you.

Happy Carving!
Desiree Hajny

Lobo Lope (gray wolf) by Desiree Hajny

Untitled (coyote)
by Desiree Hajny

Mama Knows Best (red fox and kits) by
Desiree Hajny

Untitled (wolf) by Desiree Hajny

Intermission (wolf and cubs) by Desiree Hajny

In Protest (wolf and cubs)
by Desiree Hajny

Carving Wolves, Foxes and Coyotes

Patience Worn Thin (gray wolf and cubs) by Desiree Hajny

High Plains Drifter
(coyote)
by Desiree Hajny

Sleepy Head (fox kit)
by Desiree Hajny

Arctic Cuddle
(Arctic fox)
by Desiree Hajny

Carving Wolves, Foxes and Coyotes

Fox Tale (fox) by Desiree Hajny

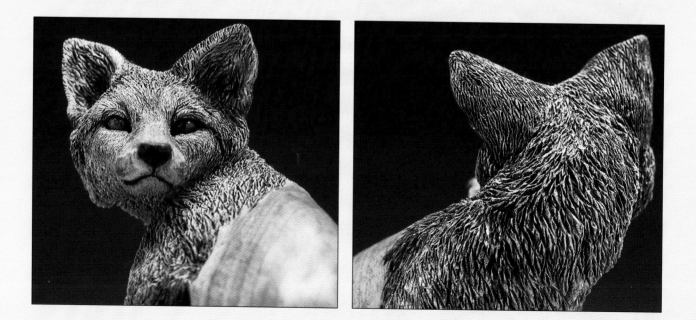

Carving Wolves, Foxes and Coyotes

Chapter One

Research

As I become older it becomes apparent to me that those who are truly successful in their ventures are people that are excited about what they do. The enthusiasm they carry for their particular endeavors carries over to whatever it is that they may be pursuing at the time. I think an enthusiastic attitude is paramount in attempting to carve a piece that will not only be significant to you, but hopefully to others who are viewing your work.

Research becomes a vital key in the overall process of the carving you are working on; as important as the carving is finishing, painting (if you choose to go this route), and design. A carving that possesses flaws in its overall presentation because of lack of research will never be as effective as one that has been thoroughly delved into and in which the intricacies and nuances of a particular subject are brought forth accurately.

I'm sure the question of "artistic license" comes into play for some regarding the above. Artistic license can sometimes be an abused term. My personal interpretation of artistic license is knowing your subject thoroughly and applying this knowledge to stretch, simplify, or delete—but not to lose the essence of your particular subject.

Some key factors to consider when choosing a subject:

1. Analyze the ideas, experiences, and feelings about the subject that are significant to you.

2. Select the ideas, experiences, and feelings that you believe to be most important.

3. Relate the ideas through the use of materials (media) in an orderly arrangement (design), which emphasizes reality in a personal way (style).

The feeling of a carving subject goes to waste unless backed by knowledge about the subject. You must understand and study your subject. I was made aware of this years back when I was teaching high school art classes. There were things that were significant to me that did not interest the students at all. When I introduced carving as a unit of study it perked some interest because most of the boys, and some girls, carried pocket knives to school as part of their attire because it related to being on the ranch. The knives were necessary for the work they were accustomed to doing. This interest was further elicited when the students were given their choice of what to carve. I learned more about rodeo, cowboys, steers, bulls, and horses than I could have imagined. These weren't subjects that I was particularly interested in delving into, but the students were.

This same application can assist you in reaching your potential. The message is, "If it doesn't interest you, look for something that does." This became painfully clear to me when I was commissioned to do an eagle some years back. For starters I didn't possess the knowledge to do the project justice, nor did I have the desire to learn about it. So, the eagle ended up looking more like a puppet eagle on a children's television show than a real, live eagle. I kept it as a reminder to make sure I didn't try to undertake something I wasn't interested in doing.

Being excited about your project cannot be stressed enough. Once you have decided what it is you want to do, obtain as much information about your subject as possible. You can read about it, rent videos, draw your ideas…. Museums and libraries are wonderful resources. Computers are an excellent resource for information, and they are becoming more user-friendly.

I love to go to zoos to watch my subjects move. When I watch the animal in question, I try to focus on different parts of the subject and think of how I will synthesize these different aspects into my finished product. How the hip tilts… Backbone and lumbar movements… How one body part moves while another is moving… The study of shapes and curves is important to ensure the flow of the design, whether it is stylized, realistic or cartoon-like. If carving people interests you, visiting shopping malls, going to fairs, sitting in airports,

and attending sporting events will provide you not only with a variety of different looks, but also with a wide variety of emotional responses.

When I am carving a canine, I put our dog to work. I observe her, and if I have a question about how one part of her body moves in conjunction with another, I try to pose her in that particular position. I get some strange glances from her, but this is an interesting and realistic manner of checking into a particular question I may have.

Taxidermy mounts are good reference, but keep in mind that a taxidermy mount is not always accurate when compared to the live animal. Sometimes the skins mounted are old and cracking. Sometimes the taxidermist may not have done his or her homework. But there is

Red Wolf

usually consistency in the nosepads, claws, dewclaws, hooves, antlers and ears. (See the sidebar on taxidermy photos later in this section for some examples where the taxidermist has done a beautiful job.)

Don't be afraid to search deeper into your subject. You might touch upon a certain feature of the subject that makes your mouth water or that gives you goosebumps. Several years back I was working on a project that held special interest to me. I was carving a wolf mother and her pups. This carving had significance for me because the carving was a gift to my mother and the pups represented each of my brothers and myself. It was enjoyable and made the carving much more meaningful to me to give features to each of the pups that reminded me of each of my brothers and myself.

I've included a photo of the piece, *Patience Worn Thin*, in the gallery section. As you can see, one of the puppies is off on his own, one is getting reprimanded, one is barking and making a lot of noise (Can you guess whom this represents?), and the other is observing the other pups. Of course there is a huge difference of opinion among my brothers and myself which pup represents which child in the family. Not to mention what my mother thinks!

Sketch ideas. These sketches will aid in the process of visualization in planning your carving. In planning a successful carving, one must have basic knowledge of the structure of the forms to be used in order to create the finished product. These sketches can be considered a "rehearsal" for the carving process. Creating ideas and redrawing them will help with the

Gray Wolf

application stage to the carving. Several sketches sometimes are combined together to make one idea.

For those of you who feel you can't draw, try using clay for your "sketching." You can twist and turn the clay until you get what you want. Not everyone possesses the ability to visualize three-dimensional works from two-dimensional renditions. The clay works well for those that have a strength in the tactile-kinesthetic area.

Ideas feed on other ideas. Bounce your ideas off others and get reactions from a spouse, parent, a best friend, or someone else who will be honest with you. If you can get by the initial shock of a possible critique, sometimes you can gain some valuable input.

The key point in dealing with research of your project is to undertake a subject that is of interest to you and that will be of interest for the duration of the project. If not, you may end up with another puppet-like eagle!

Taxidermy as Reference

Taxidermy mounts are good reference, but sometimes a mount is not always true to life.

Face

When using a taxidermy mount, make sure that the skins are in good shape and that the underlying muscle structure is accurately represented.

I have included several photos of a mounted gray fox in this chapter because I felt the taxidermist has done his homework and done a very effective job in his final presentation of the pose. What makes this effective? From the side view and back view photos you can see that the composition is pleasing to the eye. The tail leads the viewer gently into the animal and slowly spirals into the gaze of a beautiful face.

A close-up of the face shows that there aren't any droops, and the bilateral symmetry of the face is well executed. It actually appears as if the animal is looking at you. In the close-up of the back legs, the muscle structure is correct and the legs are pushed under the body, which allows for correct balance of the animal. (Mounts courtesy of Rick's Taxidermy & Wildlife Art, Clifton, Colorado; photos by Tam Kline.)

Back view

Side view

Hind quarters

Wolves

The timber wolf and the red wolf are two North American wolf species. The adult timber wolf can measure up to six and one half feet in length and reach a weight of one hundred seventy-five pounds. The red wolf is smaller than the gray wolf. There is an incredible variety of colors and fur patterns in the wolf family. The colors of the fur may blend in with the background colors in the habitat. Wolves that spend a lot of time in dark forests many times have dark fur. In places where there are many differ-

ent colored plants, the fur of the wolf may be many different colors. For protection against rain or snow, the wolf has three capes of fur on its back. Water runs off these capes in much the same manner that a raincoat repels rain. The winter coat is thicker and sometimes paler than the summer coat.

A wolf's hearing is so acute it can hear another wolf howling from as far away as several miles. It can easily tell from which direction a sound is coming. A wolf's sense of smell is its strongest sense. It can detect some scents from over one mile away. Its sense of sight is

Kits and Pups

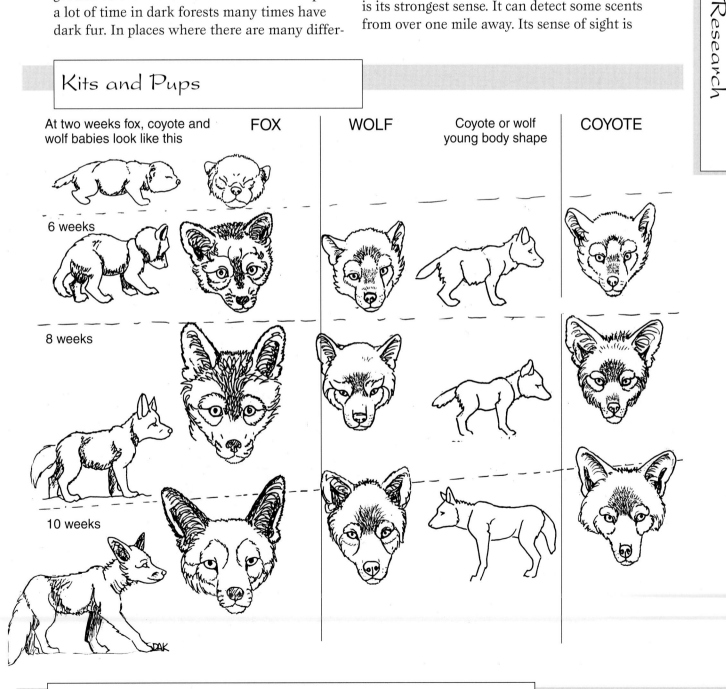

At two weeks fox, coyote and wolf babies look like this

FOX

WOLF

Coyote or wolf young body shape

COYOTE

6 weeks

8 weeks

10 weeks

DAK

Body Language

SUBMISSION

ear back

tail tucked

I'M BOSS

ears forward

puff up

tail up

teeth bared

WANT TO PLAY?

ear back

mouth open or shut

FRIGHTENED

ear back

backing off

tail tucked

YOU'RE THE BOSS

flat ear

back arched

tail tucked

Carving Wolves, Foxes and Coyotes

probably its weakest sense. Its eyes are set into the eye sockets at an angle to see forward while they sniff the ground in order to see movement.

Its teeth are similar to that of other carnivores. The canines, the largest pointed teeth, are used for grabbing and holding prey. The carnassial teeth, those in the jaw, are used for slicing food into pieces small enough to swallow. The incisors are used to pick meat off the bones. There are five toes on a wolf's front feet, one being the dew claw (which is located on the inside of the upper part of the foot...like a thumb) and four on the rear feet (in some rare cases dew claws have been found on the rear feet). The foot of a wolf can be very big, up to five inches long. A wolf runs on its toes. This lengthens the animal's legs and allows it to run faster.

Wolves live in a variety of places: prairies, forestlands, swamps, and all but the highest of mountains. Their prey consists of what is readily available and what is easiest to catch. A wolf will eat anything from small animals to birds, and a pack may attack reindeer, sheep, moose, and other large mammals, usually taking weak, old, or very young for easy capture. If there isn't any live prey available, it may feed on carrion. After acquiring its prey, an adult wolf may eat up to twenty pounds of meat at once.

The breeding season is in the spring and the litter may range from one to eleven pups, with the average being six. The pups are blind at birth and weigh around one pound. The young are protected in dens that may extend as far back as thirty feet and slope upward to prevent

Expressions

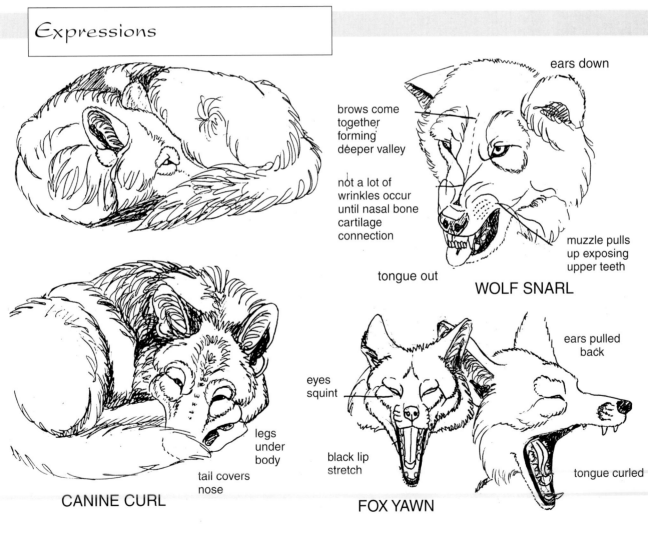

ears down

brows come together forming deeper valley

not a lot of wrinkles occur until nasal bone cartilage connection

tongue out

muzzle pulls up exposing upper teeth

WOLF SNARL

legs under body

tail covers nose

CANINE CURL

eyes squint

black lip stretch

ears pulled back

tongue curled

FOX YAWN

Chapter One

rain from coming into it. A wolf may use another animal's den if it is available. The pups are walking at two weeks and playing at the entrance of the den at about three weeks.

A wolf pack consists of a mother, father, young, and close relatives and has a very definite social order. The territory is marked by urine and feces and is very well defended. The leader, or alpha male is usually the strongest and largest of the males. His mate is the alpha female.

Wolves are able to live in a wider variety of climates and habitats than most other animals. The gray, or timber wolf lives in North America, Europe, and Asia. The red wolf can be found in Texas and the Southeastern United States. Wolves are abundant in Eastern Europe

and Asia. There are smaller populations in Western Europe. The numbers in North America have been greatly diminished. The largest numbers exist in Canada and Alaska, with smaller numbers in Minnesota and Mexico.

Wolf Walk

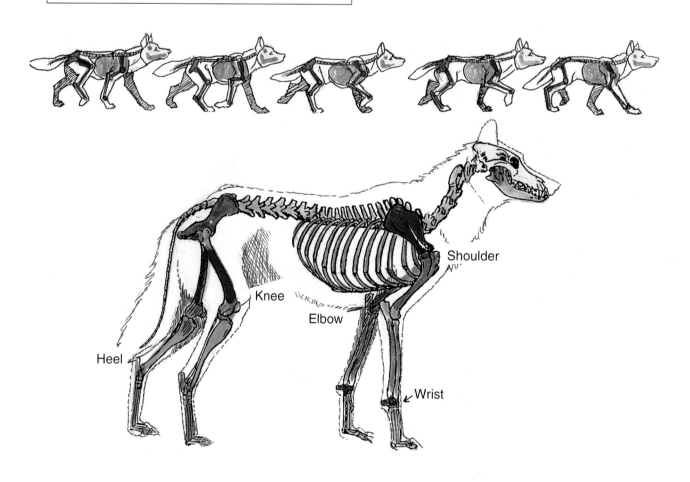

Shoulder

Knee

Elbow

Heel

Wrist

Carving Wolves, Foxes and Coyotes

Fox

The fox is the smallest of the dog family. It can be found in America, Eurasia, and Africa. There are twenty-one different subspecies of the fox, and their habitats range from the forest to chaparral to desert.

Fox are swift, agile runners and can reach

speeds of up to thirty miles per hour. The fox feeds on mice, voles, rabbits, bird's eggs, fruit, large insects, and carrion. Because of the small size of its prey, the fox is a solitary hunter. Its territory is normally a range of about three square miles.

The most common type of fox is the red fox. It lives throughout most of North America, all of Europe, most of Asia and North Africa, India, and Japan. An adult usually weighs eight to fifteen pounds and is twenty-two to twenty-five inches in length. The length of the tail of an adult can be fourteen to sixteen inches.

The red fox flourished when the pioneers first arrived in America. The land was cleared for farms and the open fields were ideal for hunting grounds. Woodlots gave protection in the winter, and the other predators left the area.

Red fox aren't much taller than a basset hound. The males are larger than the females. The fox in the south are smaller than the northern variety. The red fox in the north need

extra weight to protect their bodies from the cold. The skin and fur are also thicker, which give it a larger look.

The tail of the fox is as long as its body. Its legs are black, and chest, undersides, tip of the tail and even the lower part of the muzzle are buff white. Most red foxes generally have a coppery brown color that can vary from silvery to black. The red fox is the only fox to have a white tip on the end of its tail. Some even have cross patterns of brown or black on their back. These animals are referred to as cross fox.

A double thick coat of fur keeps the fox warm. Long, smooth guard hairs cover the underfur. The guard hairs act like a waterproof windbreaker and serve to keep out water as well as the cold wind. The woolly underfur has much the same effect as long underwear. On a cold day a fox will look for a place out of the wind, perhaps a hollow at the edge of a snow bank. It will curl up into a tight ball and fold its tail over its nose and paws.

The feet of the fox are unique in that they have fur between the foot pads, which allows for better grip on ice and snow. They also have semi-retractable claws, similar to those of a cat. They are the only known members of the dog family that can climb trees.

The fox has earned its reputation as being a

sly animal. It pulls tricks to escape enemies, from leading the enemy through a manure pile or along a tiny balanced log, to a sticky trip through a patch of raspberries. Its sense of

Pennsylvania Game Commission

Pennsylvania Game Commission

smell is so keen, a fox can find a mouse under the snow. It also possesses sharp eyesight, and has a vertical pupil, much like a cat, and good ears. A fox can detect a small movement in the grass or the smell of a tiny bird in a bush.

The fox has raised the eyebrows of many because it sometimes hunts farm animals and steals eggs. But, they also catch mice and other animals that destroy crops and stored grain. To catch a mouse, a fox will pounce and trap it between its front paws, much like a cat. It will also sit and freeze, waiting patiently before leaping on its prey, again cat-like. Sometimes the fox will bury food for later use.

If an intruder comes into a well-marked area and ignores this message, it will be challenged by the owner of the area. If a confrontation occurs between two foxes, they will stand on their hind paws and bite at the other's muzzle. The weaker usually crouches low with ears flat to admit defeat. The winner puffs up and struts stiffly to the sign post and remarks it.

During mating season, several males compete to win a mate. They strut back and forth and occasionally fight. Often the male and vixen will be lifetime mates. Sometimes the male has more than one vixen, but has a favorite. Mating occurs in January or February, and the gestation period is about fifty days. The vixen will produce one litter per year which averages from four to six kits. The kits weigh about two to four ounces at birth, and their

Fox Species

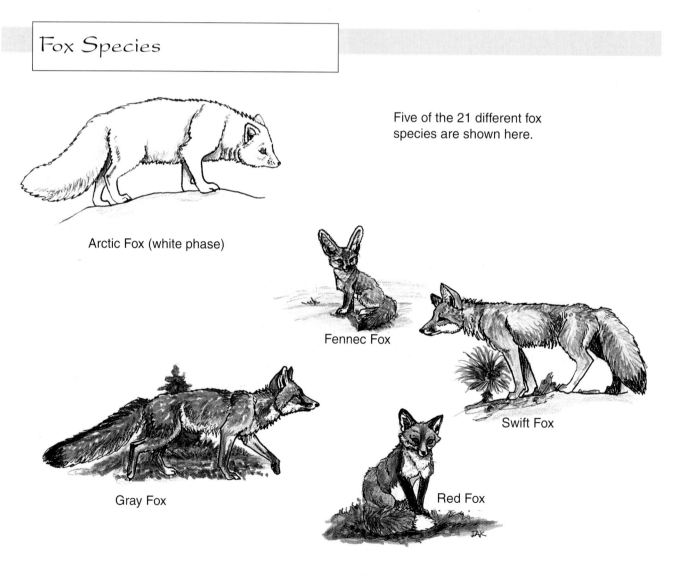

Five of the 21 different fox species are shown here.

Arctic Fox (white phase)

Fennec Fox

Swift Fox

Gray Fox

Red Fox

As the kits get older, they get rougher in their play. They stalk and pounce on each other as well as butterflies and beetles. The parents bring in mice and voles and the young learn to fight over, toss, and tear, before eating. By early fall they are three-fourth adult size. The parents leave and shortly after the kits will also. The parents won't meet again until the next mating season.

Among the other foxes the gray fox is a little smaller than the red fox, and its coat of coarse, pepper-and-salt gray hair is of less commercial value. It can be found in southern Canada to northern South America and lives mostly in forests and dry bush country. The swift fox is a shy, fast, nocturnal animal that lives in the Great Plains of southern Canada and northern United States. Known as the kit fox, it is about two-thirds the size of the red fox. The arctic fox

eyes will open on about the tenth day.

As the time for birth approaches, the parents search for a good area for a den. Foxes aren't great diggers so they scout out an old den from another animal, or a small cave, or even a hollow tree. The vixen will make modifications to enlarge it. One entrance will face the south to help keep the den warm. The main entrance usually has a clearing around it that serves as a playground for the kits, which will leave the den at about four to five weeks. The fox will use the den yearly and have more than one for safety purposes.

The male isn't allowed into the den with mother and kits until the kits eyes have opened. His role is to gather food for the vixen and serve as a guard. When the kits leave the den for the first time they are shy and scurry back to the den if something scares them, even the rustling of leaves.

Chapter One

ranges throughout the Arctic and is often found on ice fields that are quite far from the mainland. The coat is white in winter, and brown in summer. A small percentage of arctic fox have blue coats. Because of the frigid areas they inhabit, the ears of the arctic fox are short, heavily furred, and rounded, which allows heat to remain more effectively in this area.

The red fox may go through dramatic color changes: the silver phase (shown here); the cross fox, which sports a dark stripe of hair extending down the center of the back that is crossed at the shoulders by another dark stripe; and the black fox, which has a high concentration or dark or black pigment in the fur. Regardless of the color phase, the red fox always has a white tail tip.

The red fox will shed its coat in the winter. It measures 22-25 inches long, not including a tail of 14 to 16 inches, and weighs 8 to 15 pounds.

Fox Run

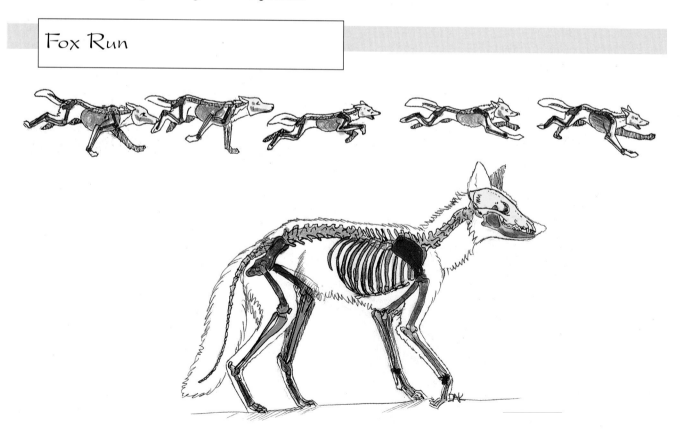

Carving Wolves, Foxes and Coyotes

Coyote

The coyote is perhaps best known for its howls that pierce the evening hours. It is most active at night, but also is present at dawn or dusk. Besides howling, the coyote is also good at barking, growling, wailing, and squealing. For a form of non-spoken communication, the coyote possesses a gland at the base of its tail that emits a scent that is used to alert other coyotes whether they be friend or foe.

Ohio Department of Natural Resources

The coyote is closely related to the wolf, with a body length of about four feet, from tip of nose to tail tip. The coat of the coyote consists of two layers. The outer layer is coarse and is used as a repellent for moisture. The under coat is also thick and provides the lining to trap in body heat. The coyote's coat is made of four colors; gray, yellow, black, and white. The overall color of the animal varies depending on the season and locale of the animal.

The coyote can swim if it has to and is an excellent jumper, reaching distances of twelve feet. The territory of a coyote consists of well-worn trails. A coyote will mark the borders of its territory to keep other coyotes out.

Coyotes range from Panama to the north slope of Alaska. They can be found in every state except Hawaii. The eastern coyote is considered a subspecies of the western variety. This animal is about twenty-five percent larger than its western counterpart. The eastern coyote has moved into the suburban areas of New York, New Jersey, Pennsylvania, and Connecticut.

A coyote has relatively poor eyesight, but this deficiency is compensated by its senses of sight and hearing. A coyote will eat carrion, birds, large insects, rodents, and rabbits. If it can't find food, many times it will eat plants. A coyote is able to open its mouth wider than a wolf or domesticated dog.

Hunting is done primarily alone or in relays. However, as many as ten coyotes have been observed stalking a large animal such as a deer. The ability to run up to forty miles per hour and change directions quickly are valuable assets in acquiring food or escaping from other predators.

A coyote will eat an already dead animal if it is available, and may wait for another animal such as a badger to dig out a mouse and then chase the badger's prey down itself. Coyotes have been observed playing dead, and when a crow comes to investigate have captured the bird.

The mating usually occurs in February. The male and female usually stay together for years. To attract mates, the males have howling contests, which frequently turn into fights, with the female usually picking the winner as her mate. The loser of this contest picks up the same routine with another male.

After the female has chosen her new mate she will not tolerate other females around her male. Even the babysitting females (usually from the young from the year before) are sometimes treated badly by the female—even if it is perhaps her own daughter.

The female searches for the den. Once a den is established, it usually is used again the following year. A coyote will use abandoned dens and adapt them to fit their needs. Their dens are normally about nine feet long. Alternate dens are also established, in the event of emergency. Old caves or hollow logs are also sources

Coyote leg poses

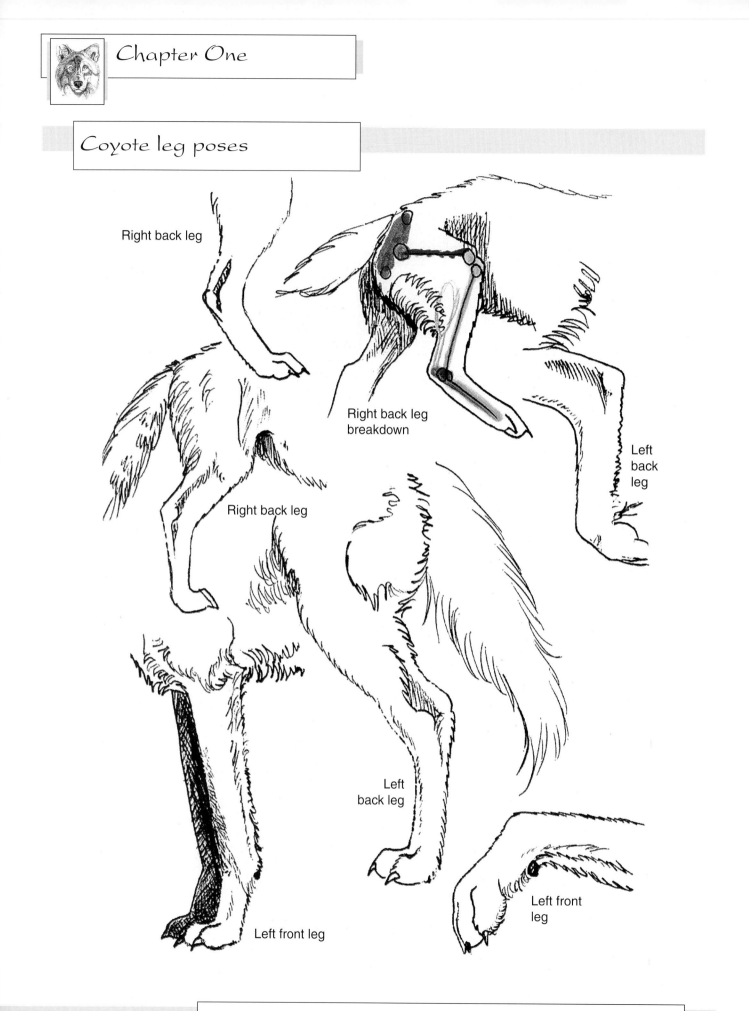

Right back leg

Right back leg
breakdown

Left
back
leg

Right back leg

Left
back leg

Left front
leg

Left front leg

for dens.

The mother does a thorough cleaning of the den before the pups are born. The gestation period is normally two months. A litter consists normally of five to seven pups, with numbers as large as nineteen being recorded. The eyes of the young will not open for the first two weeks. For the first month of their lives, the young will survive on mother's milk.

When they are able, the young will gather at the entrance of the den and play, with the mother in close proximity. If she takes note of a predator, she will quickly warn the young and they will make their way into the den. A mother was observed using a fake limp to lure a predator away from her young.

The father doesn't see the pups for the first two months. His role during this time is to protect the den and bring in food to the entrance for the mother. Both parents will teach the young how to hunt. In the fall, when the pups have reached about twenty pounds, they will leave.

Coyotes can live about ten to twelve years, with recorded lengths of thirty years in captivity.

Coyotes are occasionally active during the day, but most are nocturnal, being very active at dusk and at dawn. Daytime activity increases in spring and summer during the pup-rearing months.

Coyote Jog

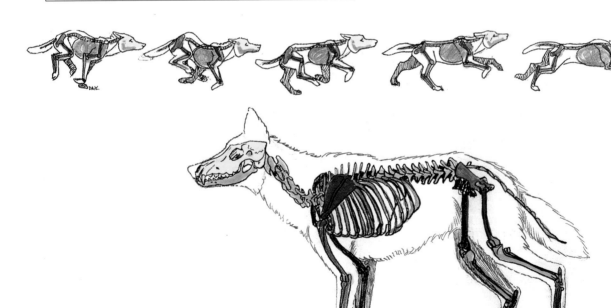

Expressions

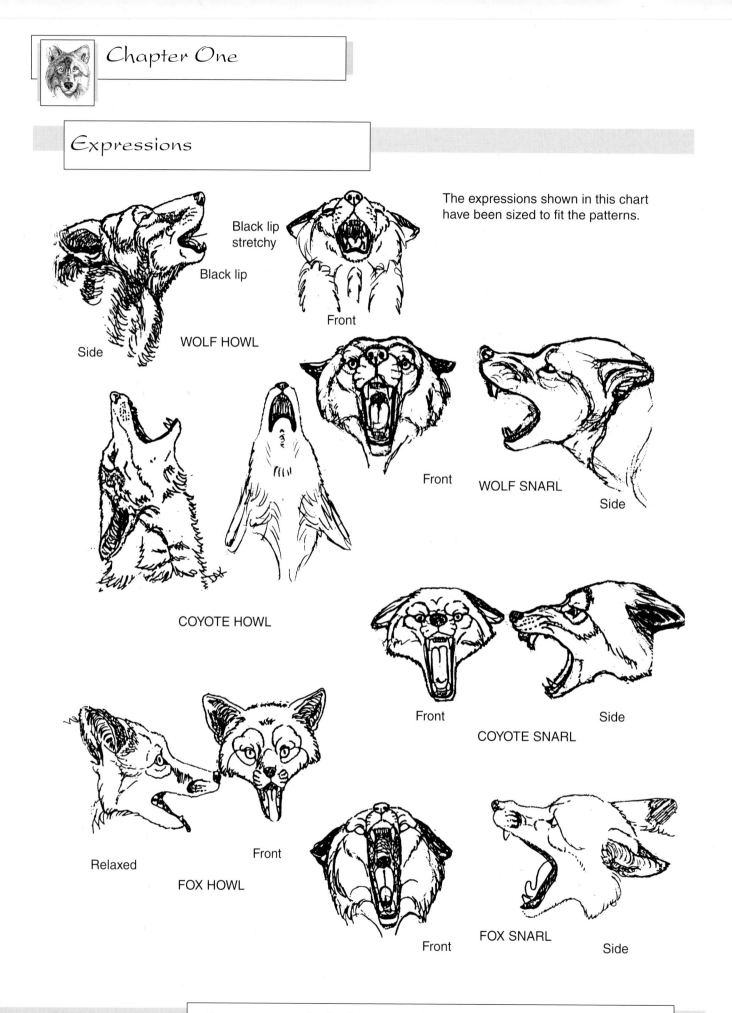

The expressions shown in this chart have been sized to fit the patterns.

Black lip stretchy

Black lip

Side

Front

WOLF HOWL

Front   WOLF SNARL

Side

COYOTE HOWL

Front   Side

COYOTE SNARL

Relaxed   Front

FOX HOWL

Front   FOX SNARL   Side

Female coyotes are exceptional mothers. They bear two to 11 pups, born during April and May, and keep more than one den in case an emergency arises that requires them to move their pups.

The average coyote stands about 18 to 24 inches tall and measures between 41 and 53 inches in length. Males generally weigh about 35 pounds, with the females weighing about five pounds less.

The coyote has exceptional senses of smell, sight and hearing. The eyes are usually yellow, though some coyotes have been found with brown eyes.

Coyotes mark their territories with urine and droppings. The territory that a mated pair covers varies greatly depending on the area of the country, the availability of food and the number of other coyotes in the area. The average territory measures from three to 12 square miles.

The color of a coyote's coat varies with each animal, but reddish gray is most common. Older animals generally have darker, more reddish coats; younger coyotes are more gray.

Coyotes are omnivorous and will eat whatever is readily available. Small mammals and an occasional bird make-up the bulk of the coyotes' diets.

The arctic fox lives in the treeless coastal areas of Alaska from the Aleutian Islands north to Point Barrow and east and west of the Canadian border. In the summer, the arctic fox has a gray or blue coat; in the winter, the coat turns white. It averages six to 10 pounds and 43 inches in length including the tail.

The kit fox's specific diet varies with its range. Generally, its diet includes small mammals, such as mice, rabbits and squirrels; insects; ground-nesting birds; and vegetation.

The kit fox is endangered throughout the United States and threatened in California. Weighing only about five pounds and measuring just 30 inches, it is North America's smallest member of the canine family.

The color and texture of the kit fox's fur vary with the season and the animal's location. The most common coat colors are buff, tan and a yellowish-gray. Summer coats are tannish in color; winter coats tend to be more gray.

The kit fox is found on the desert plains from Canada to Mexico. It is considered to be a nocturnal animal, but is often seen during the day in late spring and early summer.

Foxes are opportunists and scavengers. They will eat whatever is readily available, including mice, rabbits, chickens, insects, eggs, fruits, grasses and even dead animals. Foxes may cache uneaten food by burying it in loose earth.

The gray fox is 21 to 29 inches long and its tail adds an extra 11 to 16 inches. The gray fox only weighs seven to 13 pounds, though it looks heavier due to its thick fur.

The gray fox prefers bushy areas, swampy lands and rugged mountainous terrain. Unlike the red fox, which seems to be comfortable living close to humans, the gray fox is more solitary.

The gray fox is a swift runner and can swim if it has to. It is the only member of the canine family that can climb trees.

The red wolf is named for the reddish color of its head, ears and legs, but the color of its coat varies from light tan to black. The head is broader than a

In the 1930s, only two populations of red wolves existed in the United States; one in the Ozark/Quachita Mountain region of Arkansas, Oklahoma and Missouri and the other in southern Louisiana and southeastern Texas. By 1967, the red wolf was considered an endangered species, and by 1980, extinct in the wild. Captive breeding and reintroduction programs have brought the species count to nearly 300, with one quarter of the population living in the wild.

The average red wolf weighs 45 to 80 pounds, making it smaller than the gray wolf but larger than the coyote. The red wolf hunts in a pack, with the white-tailed deer and the raccoon being the most important part of the animal's diet.

coyote's but more narrow than a gray wolf. Its long ears are a distinguishing feature.

The average Mexican wolf weighs between 50 and 90 pounds. It measures 4.5 to 5.5 feet from nose to tail and stands 26 to 32 inches at the shoulder.

Wolf pups are blind and deaf at birth and weigh about one pound. They become more playful as their sight and hearing develop, usually two to three weeks after birth. They leave the den to join the pack when they are about six weeks old.

The fur on the gray wolf's back is a silvery gray-brown color. The underparts are a tan color. In winter, the fur on the neck, shoulders and rump becomes darker in color.

The Mexican wolf is currently on the endangered species list. In 1996, 150 Mexican wolves lived in captivity with no confirmed sightings of wild animals since 1980. Plans are being made to reintroduce the Mexican wolf into areas of Arizona and New Mexico during 1998.

Tracks can easily distinguish a wolf from a dog. A wolf usually places its hind foot in the tract left by the front foot; a dog's footprints do not overlap.

Gray wolves, often called timber wolves, are the largest member of the canine family. The male gray wolf weighs an average 45 pounds; the female, 60 pounds. It measures 5 to 5.5 feet in length (including the tail) and stands 2.5 feet tall.

The gray wolf is an endangered species in the lower 48 states. It was given protection under the Endangered Species Act in 1974. Through careful monitoring, gray wolf populations are slowly beginning to increase.

Chapter Two

Technique

Canine Carving

The projects in this book are all carved from basswood. This is the wood that I feel most comfortable using. Please feel free to exercise that same option and use what is most comfortable for you.

The dimensions listed in the next paragraphs are comparable to what I have done for this book. Again, feel free to shrink or enlarge and adapt the dimensions to meet your needs. I have included plenty of information to give you the leverage to do some redesigning, including simple changes such as turning the head and more complex changes such as altering the animal's pose. Use these instructions and study the illustrations.

On all the projects the wood grain should run vertically. Cutting out the project and making sure the grain runs in the correct direction will add strength to the legs. It took me several years of carving and much gluing and repairing before I learned this.

The wolf dimensions are seven and one half inches in length, three and three quarter inches in height, and three inches in width. The wolf pup is two and three quarters inches in length, one and one half inches in height, and one inch in width.

The coyote is five and one quarter inches in length, five and one half inches in height, and two and one half (or three) inches in width. The coyote pup is three and one quarter inch in length, one and one half inches in height, and one and one quarter inches in width.

The fox is four inches in length, six inches and three quarters in height, and three and three quarters inches in width. The fox kit is three and one quarter inches in length, two inches in height (add more if you've included a base), and one inch in width.

On the above dimensions, add extra inches to the width if you are redesigning the pattern. This will give you some extra latitude to create whatever type of pose or habitat you desire.

Once you've decided which of the canine poses you are going to do, draw a side view pattern on the wood using carbon paper. You can also trace around a cut-out pattern with a pencil or knife. Tracing the pattern onto acetate and then to the block is a another method.

If you are using carbon paper to transfer your pattern to the block of wood, simply place a piece of carbon paper, carbon side down, on the block. Place your pattern on top of the carbon paper. Using a pointed object like a pen or pencil, trace along the lines of the pattern. When you remove the pattern and carbon paper, the outline will appear on the wood. Cut this out on the bandsaw. Repeat this process on the remaining sides and top of the block for carving reference.

Use the top view of the pattern to sketch in the top parts of the body on the cut-out. On either side of the cut-out, carve to those lines. At this time leave the base area alone. If you've changed the design, leave some extra wood to accommodate for the bulges and wrinkles that may be present in your subject. You should have removed enough wood so that your project has the curves and contours shown in the drawings, and those shown in your own changes.

Whenever I do a carving my first challenge is

Chapter Two

the head. If you can get the face carved to your liking, a personality will emerge. Plus, it takes some of the pressure off. I figure if the head doesn't turn out the way I want it to, it's easier for me to scrap the project at this point and start over.

From the top view, draw in using the measurements taken from the patterns. The centerpoint is vital. Pay close attention to it on the chart, especially if you have redesigned by turning the head. The circle colored light blue is the pivot point (see the illustrations on pages 30

Top Views, Head

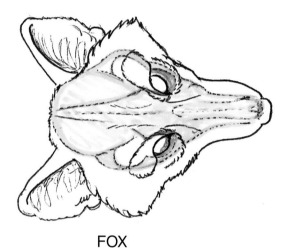

FOX

FROM TOP VIEW
angle to opening of ear from
point in front of nosepad

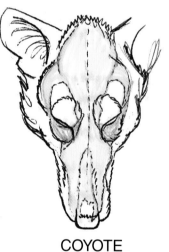

COYOTE

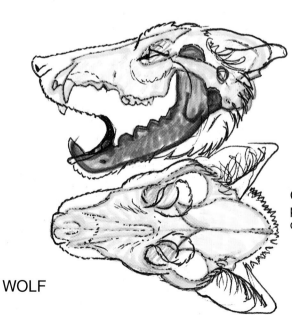

WOLF

Chin sweeps back from
pivot point (below ear
opening)

and 31).

At this point, mark in the bridge of the nose. Mark in the eye socket area. Paying close attention to the bridge of the nose and using the front and side view patterns, use gouge #6, which is a one-quarter inch gouge, on each side, tapering the nose down and behind the muzzle area. Leave the top of the bridge of the nose flat. It is important to remember that you are tapering on each side of the muzzle so the critter can see forward too. (The illustration on page 30 will help you to understand.) Canines have sockets that are set back and angled upward so they can see any movement ahead as they sniff the ground.

Gouge out the eye sockets, keeping in mind that the eyes are positioned forward and upward. Keep referring to the patterns and the illustrations of the head. The age of the canine can influence the look of the eyes. An older dog may have sagging lids and bags under its eyes. The bilateral symmetry of the eye placement of the older dog may not be as perfect as that of a younger canine. (The illustration on page 38 shows an example of this.) If your subject is a younger pup, the bilateral symmetry will allow for the eyeball placement to be at right angles to the center point. The eyeballs can be set anywhere in the socket. The sockets are always at right angles to the centerline.

The area under the cheekbones of your canine will sink in slightly. As you make these cuts, use gentle swoops, again using #5 or #6 gouge. Refer to the patterns for an accurate depth of the sweeps. On the temple area, again use a #5 or #6 gouge. This is the area between the eyes and ears. Sink in gently, again referring to the patterns.

Differentiation of depth must be considered, depending on the species you are carving and the subject's facial expression (See the illustrations on pages 14, 15 and 24). When carving pups, keep in mind that the tools you use will have the same sweeps but should be smaller in width.

When starting on the face, there are many slight differences to consider. For whichever canine you are doing refer to the illustrations on pages 35, 36, 37, 40, 41 and 44 and proceed from there. Remember to allow for changes in expressions. The front and side views are sized to fit over the patterns in this book. (For the young faces, the illustrations on page 13 will help you to decide the age.)

Anatomy

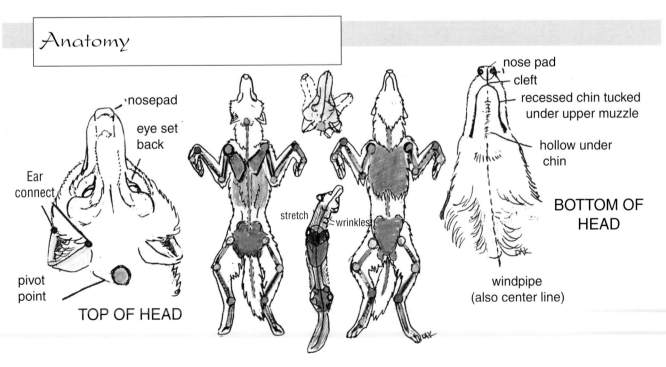

nosepad

eye set back

Ear connect

pivot point

TOP OF HEAD

stretch
wrinkles

nose pad
cleft
recessed chin tucked under upper muzzle
hollow under chin

BOTTOM OF HEAD

windpipe (also center line)

Anatomy

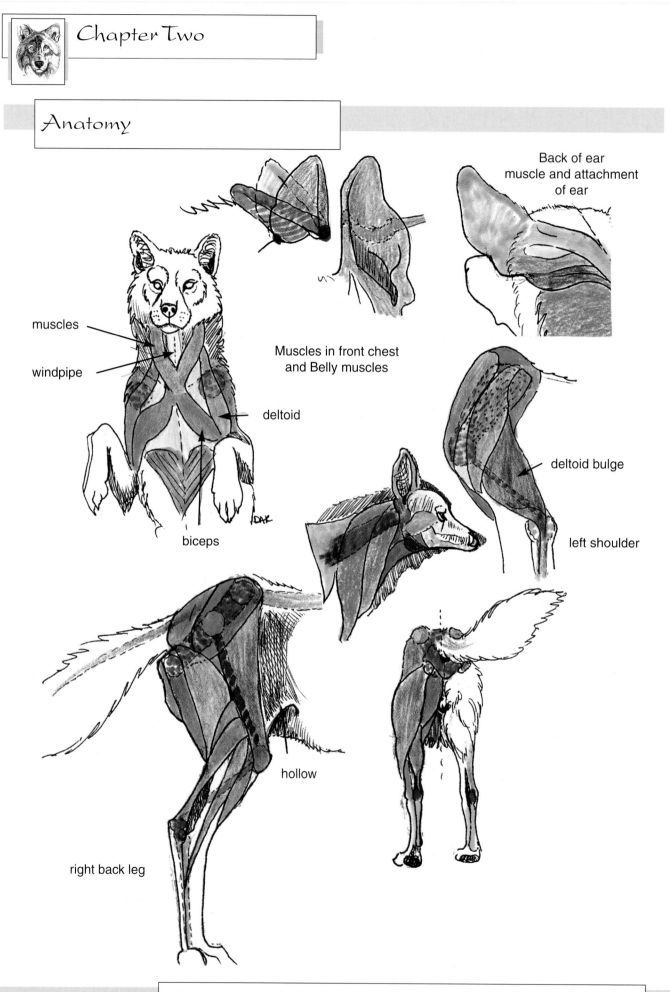

Back of ear
muscle and attachment
of ear

muscles

windpipe

Muscles in front chest
and Belly muscles

deltoid

biceps

deltoid bulge

left shoulder

hollow

right back leg

When you are ready to begin the body, use the pattern from the book (or yours if you've made adaptations). Begin by drawing in the spine. The line for the spine serves as a centerpoint. Taper in the shoulder blade area using a #4 or #5, 1/2" gouge. (Rotary carvers should try a Carbide Kutzall burr, cone-shaped, 1/4 x 3/4 x 3/8").

The shoulder blades are not fused to the backbone. The blades are connected by tendons and ligaments. Imagine these as rubber bands providing that extra stretch needed in particular positions. Take a look at the illustration on page 32 for an in-depth study on muscle structure of the shoulder blade area and front legs. Keep in mind, as the animal moves, some of these muscles bulge out or stretch. (The illustrations on pages 16, 20 and 23 are color coded to for easier understanding of the underlying structure.)

The top part of the rib cage (remember it is hanging off of the spine) is then tapered in toward the backbone, using a #4 or #5 gouge (or rotary burr, cone-shaped, 1/4 x 3/4 x 3/8"). On the back end of the shoulder blade there is a recessed area. This space allows for movement when the animal is in motion. The shoulder blades hang from the spine and sit on top of the rib cage. As the animal moves, the blades slide up and down the rib cage depending on weight distribution. (See illustrations on pages 16, 20, 23 and 34.)

The pelvis consists of six points that push the skin up. There are three points on each side of the spine. The pelvis is fused to the backbone. This puts the points at right angles to each other across the backbone, or centerpoint. When the wolf, coyote or fox is in motion, the pelvis is always at a right angle to the spine, or the center point. (See pages 16, 20, 23 and 33.).

The lumbar region and pelvis function together as the animal moves. The lumbar region refers to the spine between the end of the ribs and the pelvis. This area of the spine is

Spine Connection

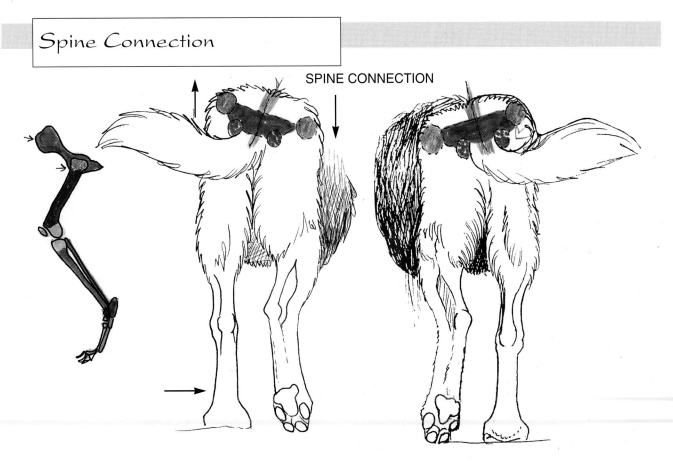

SPINE CONNECTION

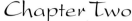
very flexible to accommodate the movement of the pelvis area (marked dark green between the orange rib cage and purple pelvis on pages 16, 20, 23 and 33). This area sinks in between the ribs and the legs from the side view to allow for back leg movement. It is the "waistline area" referred to in the illustration on page 31.

The legs hang down from the middle point of the pelvis (marked in pink in the illustrations on pages 16, 20, 23 and 31) on both sides. The belly tapers under the body and is rounded. The chest or rib cage is larger than the belly because it accommodates the large lungs for the long distances the animals need to travel. Only a pregnant female would have a belly larger than the chest cavity.

The legs that bear weight in movement angle under the body centerline. The leg that is bearing the most weight, front or back view, is pushed up. This includes the shoulder and scapula in front (see page 34). The pelvis tilts up in back (see page 33). On a lying-down pose, the legs would angle out from the body and fit around the object the dog is laying on. Be aware that the bones form straight lines. The joints allow for bending. The high points on the pelvis stick out. While shaping the body, be aware of the rib cage. Is it hanging or is it being pushed up as in the case of the sitting coyote or fox pose?

Weight Distribution

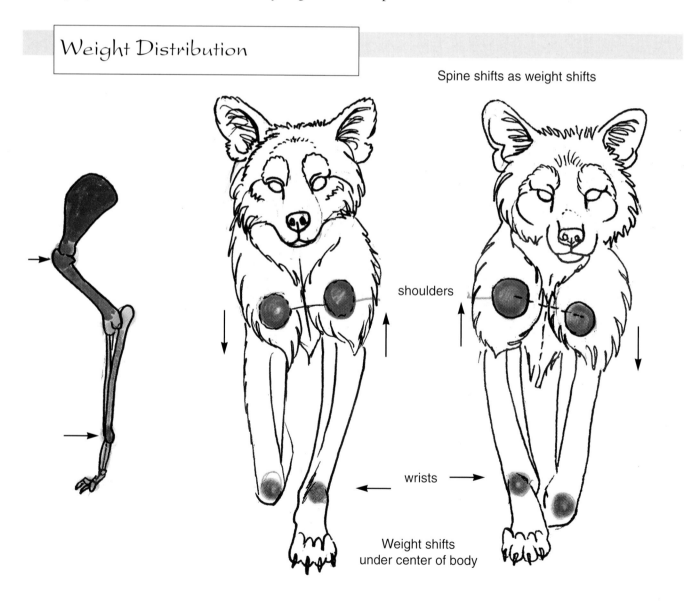

Spine shifts as weight shifts

shoulders

wrists

Weight shifts under center of body

Shape up the feet by following the illustrations on pages 39, 41 and 45. Study the illustrations on pages 16, 20, 23, 38, 42 and 46 for leg movement. Study these charts as well for leg shaping. For redesigning legs, study leg movements on these same charts.

Apply your research skills to study the structure of the species you have decided to carve. Use the illustrations on page 13 also for body shape of chosen age of pups. Keep in mind that each pose here is interchangeable. For example, either the fox or coyote can be in the same position as the wolf. The structures vary some, but can be adjusted easily in your redesigned pattern.

Throughout the charts you'll find different sketches of poses. Try incorporating these with your designs and have fun.

Wolf Head Technique

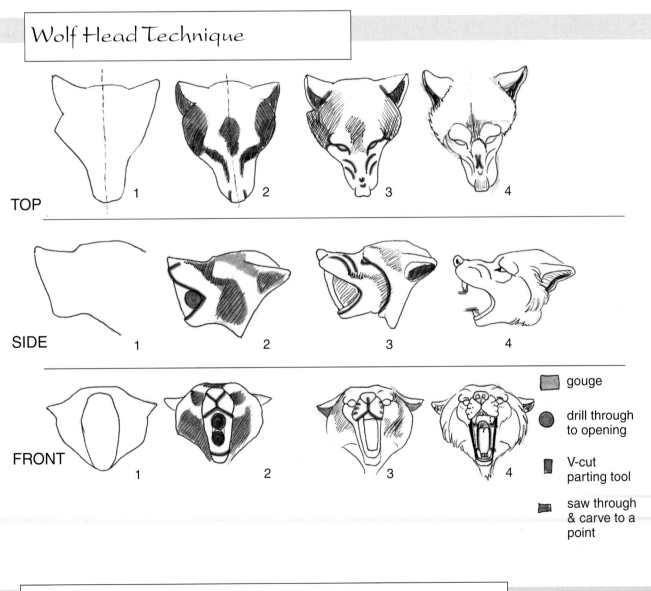

TOP 1 2 3 4

SIDE 1 2 3 4

FRONT 1 2 3 4

gouge

drill through to opening

V-cut parting tool

saw through & carve to a point

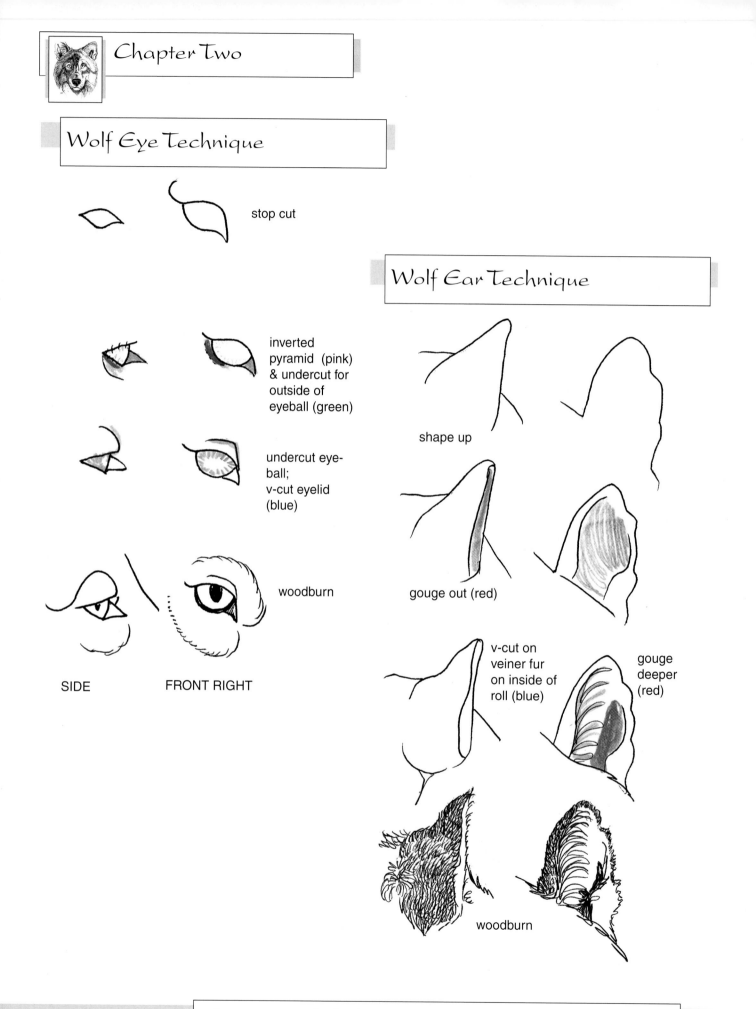

Chapter Two

Wolf Eye Technique

stop cut

inverted pyramid (pink) & undercut for outside of eyeball (green)

undercut eyeball; v-cut eyelid (blue)

woodburn

SIDE

FRONT RIGHT

Wolf Ear Technique

shape up

gouge out (red)

v-cut on veiner fur on inside of roll (blue)

gouge deeper (red)

woodburn

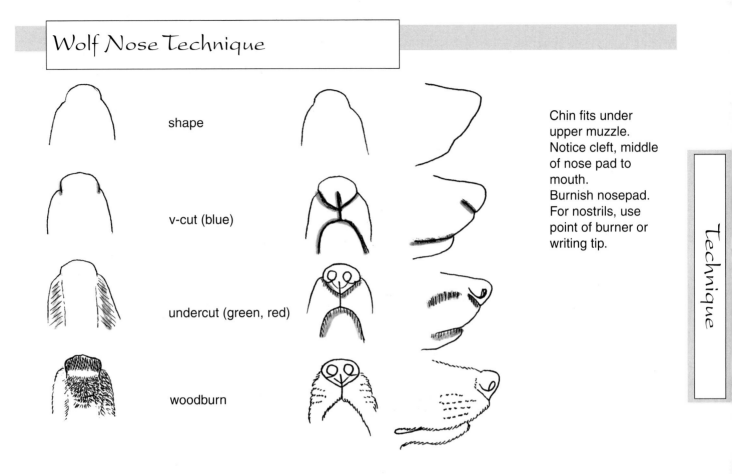

shape

v-cut (blue)

undercut (green, red)

woodburn

Chin fits under upper muzzle. Notice cleft, middle of nose pad to mouth.
Burnish nosepad. For nostrils, use point of burner or writing tip.

Technique

Wolf Hair Tract

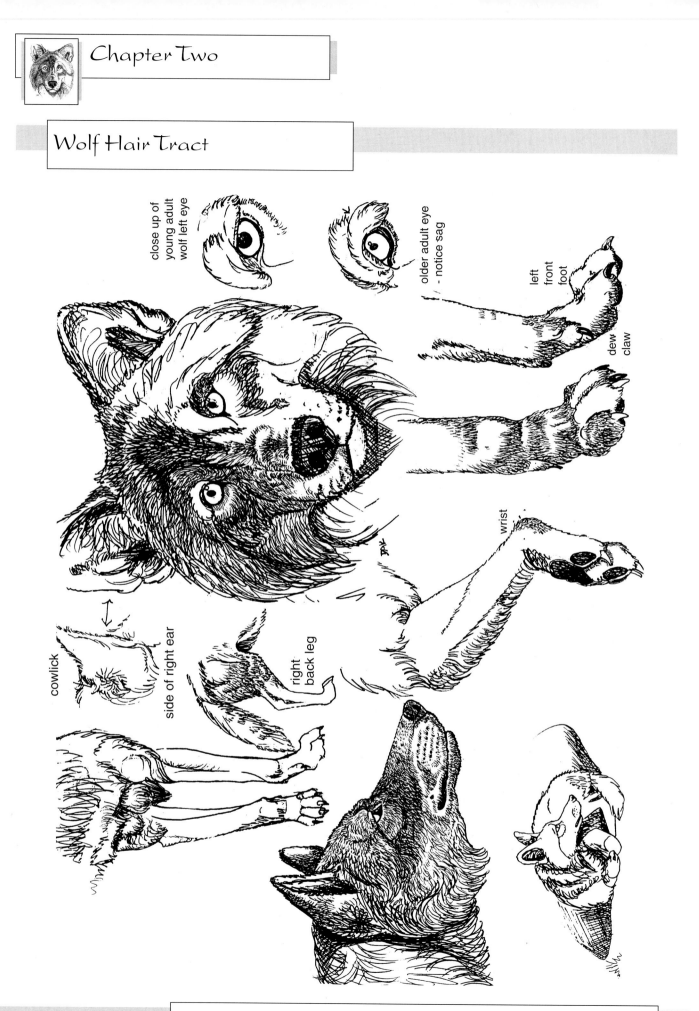

close up of young adult wolf left eye

older adult eye - notice sag

left front foot

dew claw

wrist

cowlick

side of right ear

right back leg

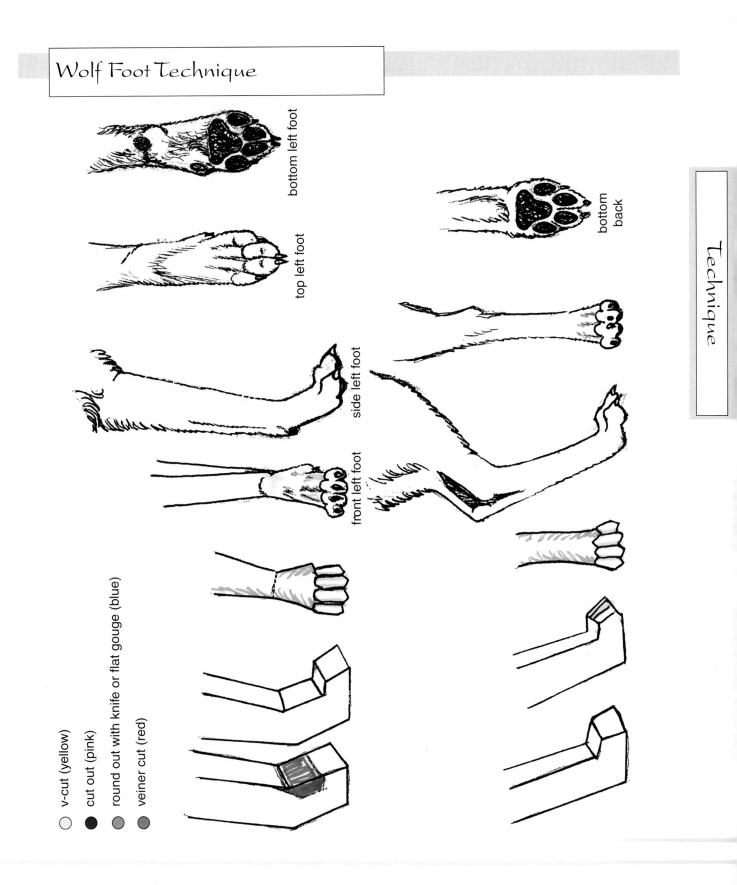

bottom left foot

top left foot

bottom back

side left foot

front left foot

○ v-cut (yellow)
● cut out (pink)
◐ round out with knife or flat gouge (blue)
◑ veiner cut (red)

Technique

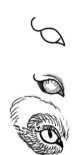

Fox Technique

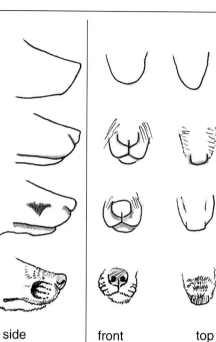

side   front   top

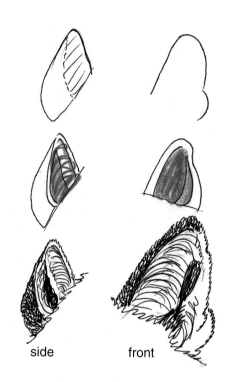

side   front

1. stop cut (knife)

2. inverted pyramid (pink) and under cut with knife (green)

3. undercut eyeball (green); v-cut lid (blue)

4. woodburn

1. shape side, front and top

2. v-cut (blue)

3. undercut (green) and gouge out nostrils using a tiny gouge or writing tip of burner

4. woodburn (nose pad- burnish)

1. shape using pattern

2. gouge out hollow of ear (red); v-cut rolls of cartilage (blue)

3. woodburn

Fox Foot Technique

- ○ v-cut (yellow)
- ● cut out (pink)
- ◐ round out with knife or flat gouge (blue)
- ◓ veiner cut (red)

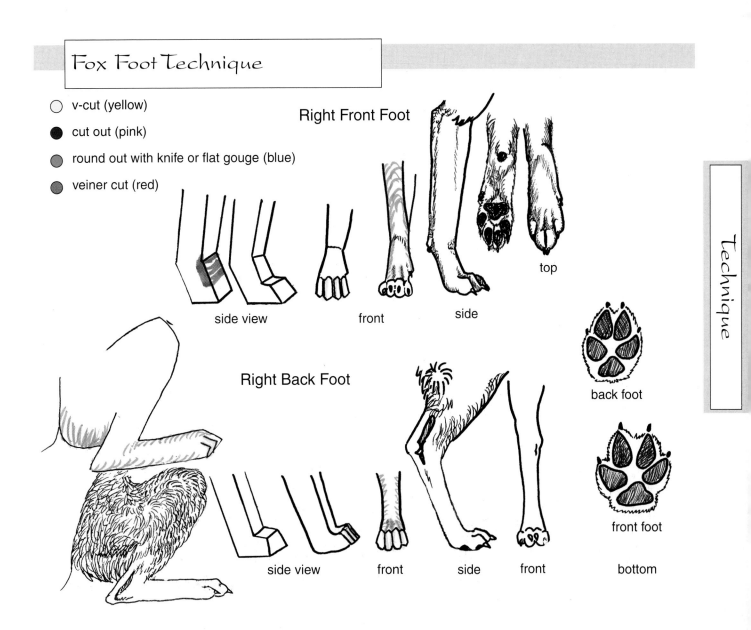

Right Front Foot

side view   front   side   top

back foot

Right Back Foot

side view   front   side   front   front foot

bottom

Fox Hair Tract

left front leg

bend

pad

Carving Wolves, Foxes and Coyotes

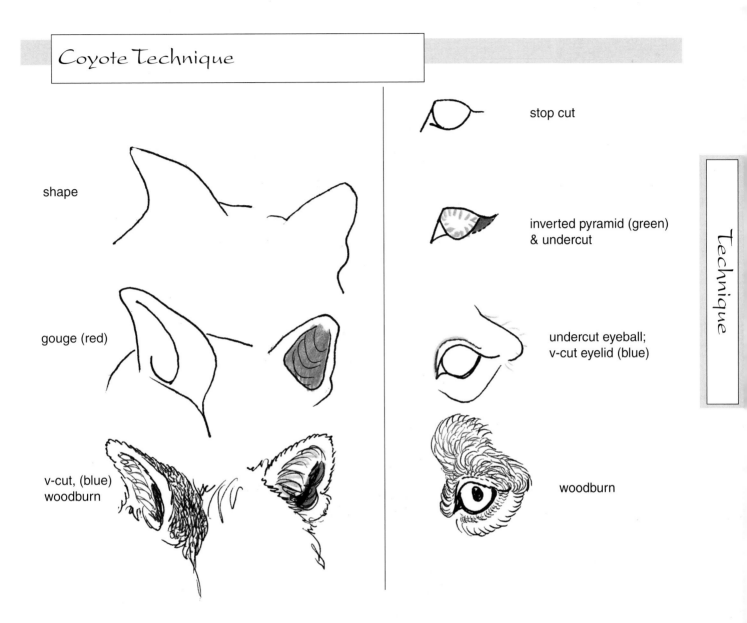

shape

gouge (red)

v-cut, (blue)
woodburn

stop cut

inverted pyramid (green)
& undercut

undercut eyeball;
v-cut eyelid (blue)

woodburn

Technique

Coyote

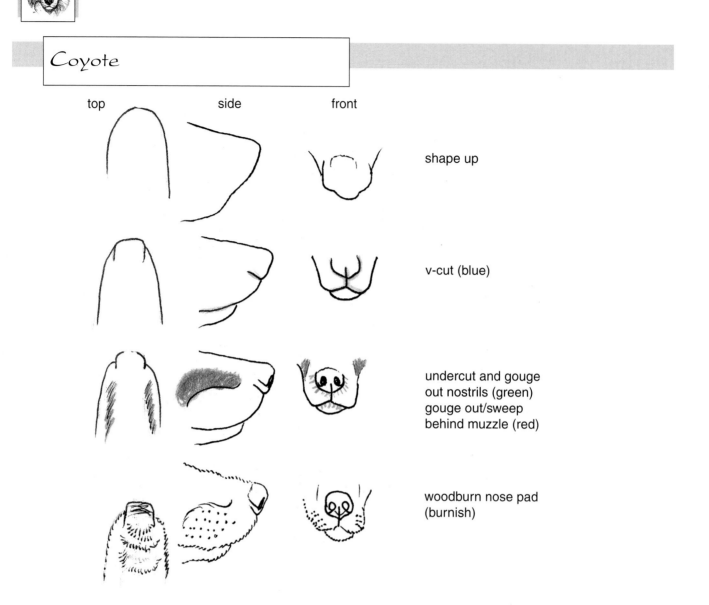

top   side   front

shape up

v-cut (blue)

undercut and gouge
out nostrils (green)
gouge out/sweep
behind muzzle (red)

woodburn nose pad
(burnish)

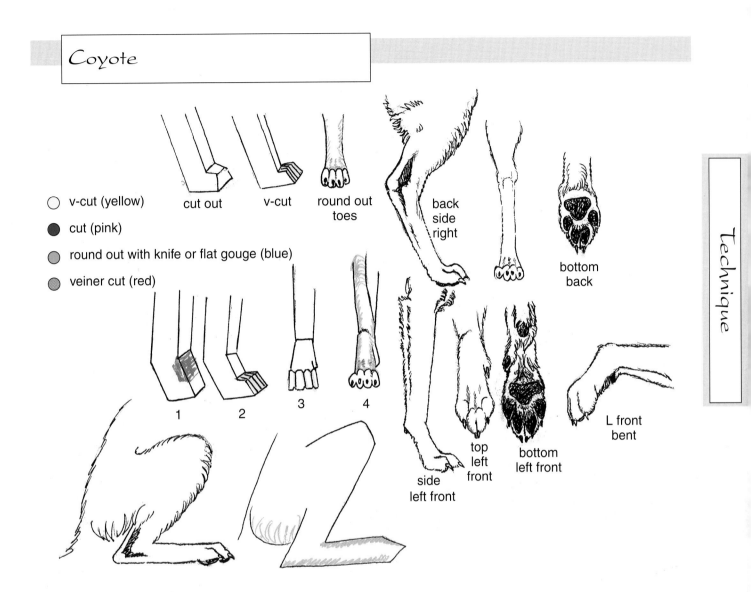

- ○ v-cut (yellow)
- ● cut (pink)
- ◑ round out with knife or flat gouge (blue)
- ◑ veiner cut (red)

cut out

v-cut

round out toes

back side right

bottom back

1

2

3

4

side left front

top left front

bottom left front

L front bent

Coyote Hair Tract

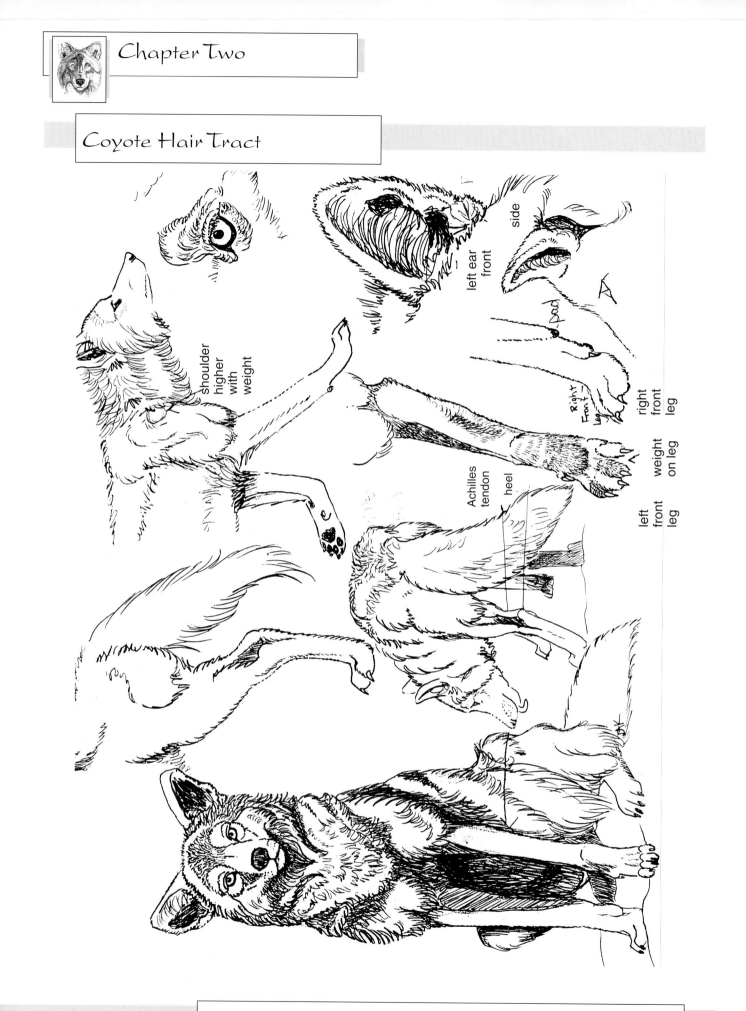

shoulder higher with weight

left ear front

side

Right Front Leg

right front leg

weight on leg

Achilles tendon

heel

left front leg

Chapter Three

Step-by-Step

Carving a Wolf

Recommended tools

Always keep in mind that it is important to use what you feel comfortable using. These are tools that I have used in this section, and there are probably tools that you may choose to better meet your needs. A photo of the finished piece appears on page 1; patterns are on pages 75 and 76.

pencil
carving knife
#7, 10 mm gouge
#8, 10 mm gouge
#8, 13mm gouge
#11, 2mm gouge
#11, 5mm gouge
#11, 7mm gouge
#11, 5mm veiner
#11, 7mm veiner

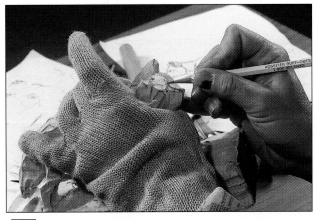

1 Measure the bridge of the nose by using the pencil width measurement taken from the pattern.

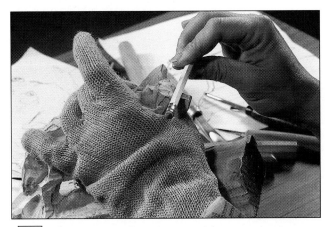

2 Using the pattern as a guide, measure two pencil widths from the tip of the nose to mark the eye socket area.

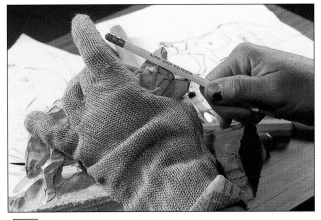

3 Mark in measurements on the head with a pencil.

4 Make sure everything is aligned before cutting.

5 Using a carving knife, cut up along the bridge of the nose to the eye socket. Roll the knife and cut outward.

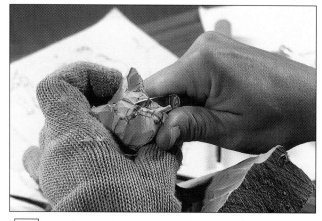

6 Using the same knife, cut inward from the outside of the socket into the previous cut.

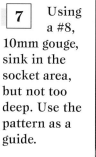 **7** Using a #8, 10mm gouge, sink in the socket area, but not too deep. Use the pattern as a guide.

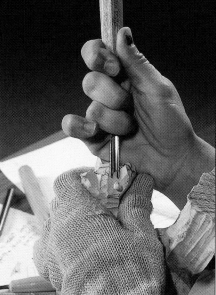

8 Carve off the sharp corners on each side of the bridge of the nose. You want the nose to have a rounded, tapered look—not squarish.

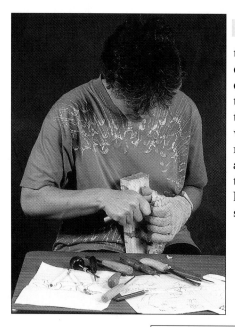

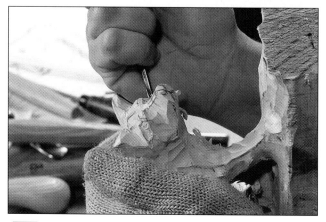

9 Using a #11, 2mm gouge, softly carve the inside part of the eye socket around the tear duct area, and push the cut from there to the side of the nose pad.

10 Stop cut on the sides of the nose pad with a carving knife. (A v-cut will also work.) Be careful not to cut on top of the nose pad.

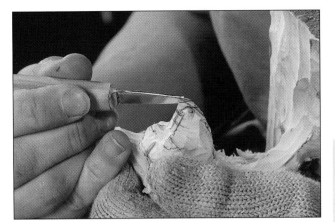

11 Undercut with the same knife around and below the nose pad.

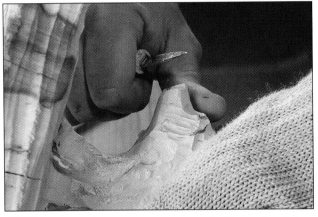

12 Taper the chin area with a knife so the chin slopes under the muzzle area.

13 Draw in the shoulder and leg area, using the pattern as your guide.

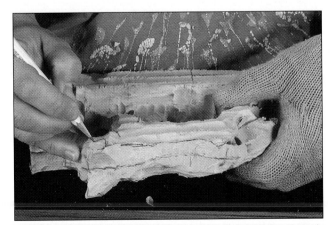

14 Notice the centerline drawn on the top view is the spine area.

15 Draw the pelvis area, using the pattern as a guide.

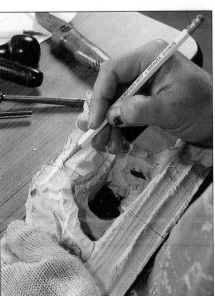

16 Refer-ring to the side view pattern, mark in and carve the excess wood from the area of the legs.

17 Using a #11, 7mm veiner, taper the neck area up to the center point. This will start the "fluffing" of the neck area.

18 Draw in the center point of the chest and run a line to the middle of the chin.

19 Again, using a #11, 7mm veiner, taper the bottom of the neck ending the cuts along the centerline. This will fluff up the neck.

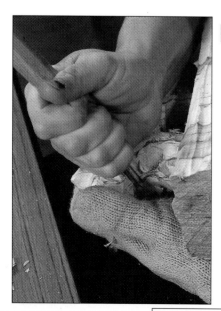

20 Using a #8, 13mm gouge, carve away the excess wood on the side of the leg. Stop at the center area.

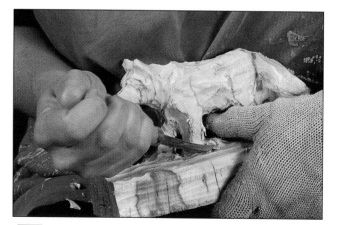

21 Study the illustration on page 34 and the pattern for the shift of weight. Draw in the front view and cut in the sides to the newly drawn lines (outside of legs) and v-cut under the leg.

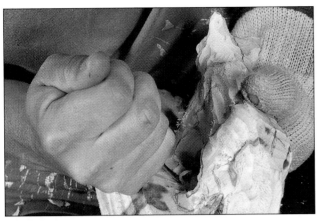

22 Using a v-cut, cut under the leg that's lifted off the base, but not completely as this could be a weak point.

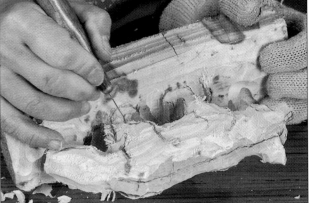

23 Draw the guides for the back leg area. Use a carving knife to stop cut the back leg.

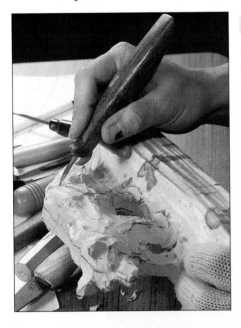

24 Stop cut the lines of the buttocks by the tail.

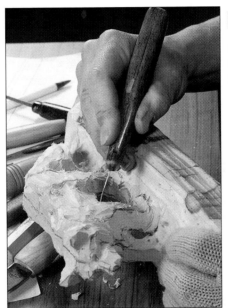

25 Stop cut and undercut the elbow area.

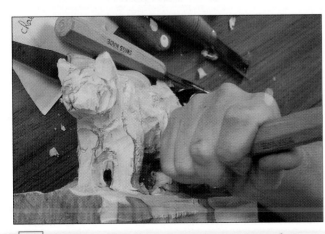

26 Using a #11, 7mm gouge, carve away the excess wood between the back legs.

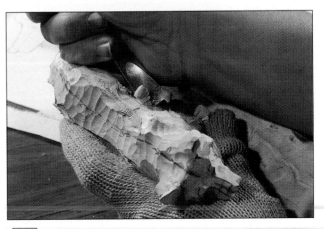

27 Sink in the area between the shoulder and rib cage with a #8, 10mm gouge.

Carving Wolves, Foxes and Coyotes

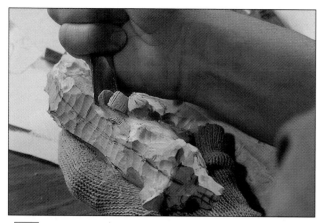

28 Using a #11, 5mm veiner, taper the rib cage area toward the spine.

29 You want the rib cage to appear to be "hanging" from the spine.

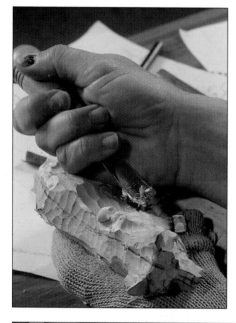

30 Taper under the belly with a #8, 10mm gouge.

31 Gouge the area behind the base of the ears with a #8, 10mm gouge.

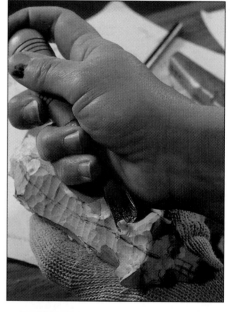

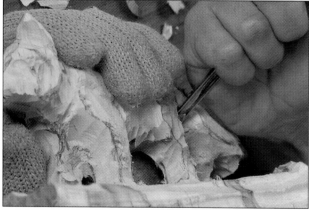

32 Using a #11, 5mm veiner, taper in the rear end area.

33 Break through the back legs, tapering the inside of the legs with a #11, 5mm veiner.

 Continue to taper in the legs using the pattern and reference materials to guide you.

35 V-cut under the flap of skin between the back leg and belly, checking the pattern.

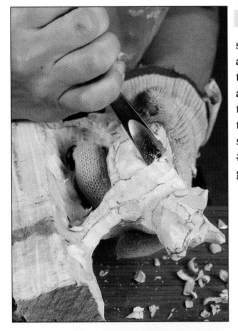

36 Continue sinking in the area behind the shoulder area. Keep tapering toward the spine, using a #8, 10mm gouge.

37 Gouge out the area of the lumbar region between the rib cage and leg.

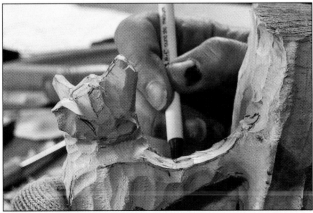

38 Mark in the features of the front leg view using the pattern and reference material.

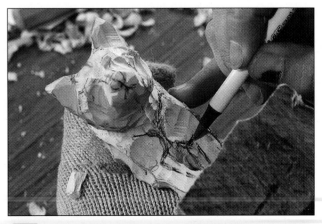

39 Continue drawing the bicep and deltoid areas.

40 Cut behind the ruff of the jowl and ear area with a #8, 10mm gouge.

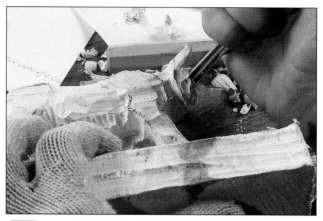

41 Continue working this area.

42 Use the carving knife to continue refining this area.

43 Cut the temple area, angled from the front brow area through the ear opening area.

44 After marking in the mouth area, use a v-cut and follow the line.

45 Make sure the chin area is tucked under the muzzle.

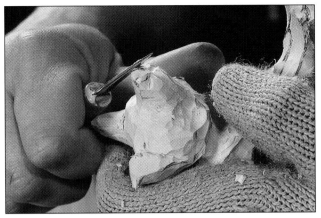

46 Round out the muzzle with a carving knife.

47 Pull the carving knife from the base of the back of the ear toward the top, tapering the ear.

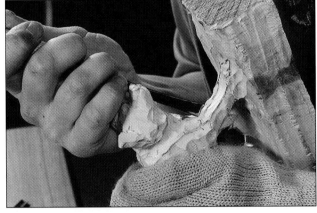

48 V-cut between the deltoid and bicep area on the center of the chest.

49 V-cut the outside of the upturned front paw.

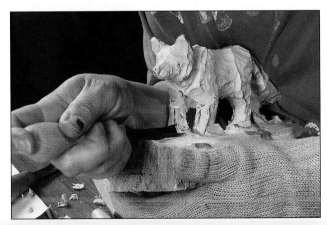

50 Using a #7, 10mm gouge, taper the inside of the front leg toward the center of the body.

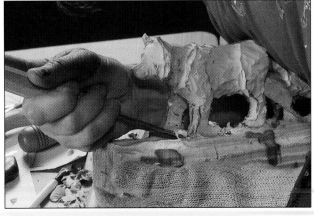

51 Cut away more wood under the upturned leg.

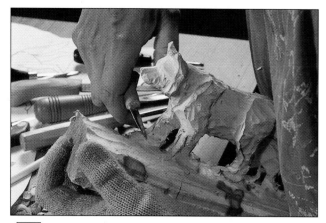

52 Cut a crisper angle with a carving knife on the inside of the front legs.

53 Round out the corners of the squared legs.

54 Cut into the sides of the paws with a #8, 13mm gouge.

55 Round out the pelvis area with a #8, 10mm gouge.

56 Using a #8, 10mm gouge, round out the top of the shoulder area so it looks like the shoulders hang from the spine.

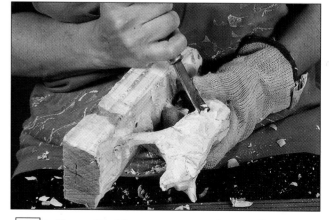

57 Use a #8, 10mm gouge to crisp up the lumbar region.

58 Check the illustrations on pages 30 and 36 and the pattern. Draw in the eyes in the socket area.

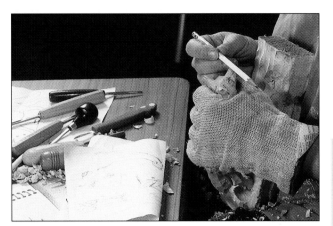

59 Check the angle to the center point.

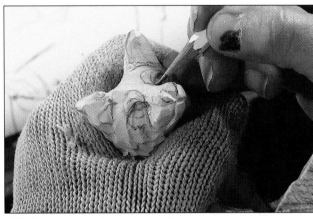

60 Draw in the brow and cheek area using the pattern or the illustrations on pages 31 and 31.

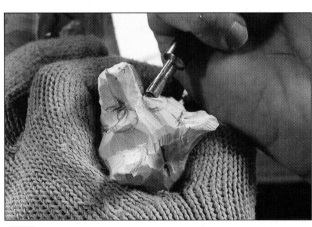

61 Gently push in eye punch or follow the steps shown on page 36.

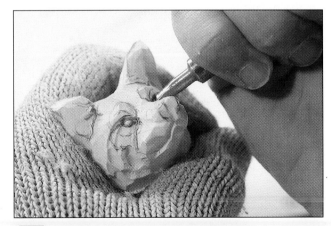

62 A close up view of the eye punch.

63 Stop cut the brow area with a carving knife.

Carving Wolves, Foxes and Coyotes

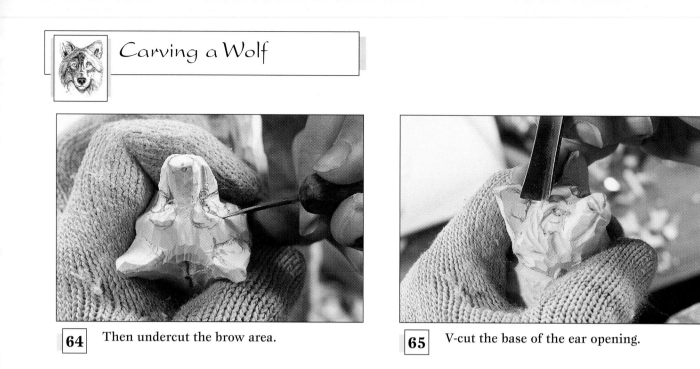

64 Then undercut the brow area.

65 V-cut the base of the ear opening.

66 V-cut the brow marking.

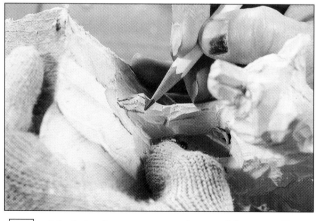

67 Gouge out the opening of the ear from the top to the v-cut using a #11, 5mm gouge.

68 Carve into the base of the ear opening with a #11, 5mm gouge.

69 Mark in the toe separations with a pencil.

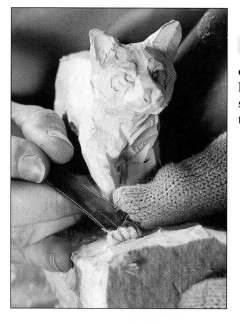

70 Use a v-cut on these lines to separate the toes.

71 V-cut around the marked dew claw. Check the illustration on page 39 or the pattern for reference.

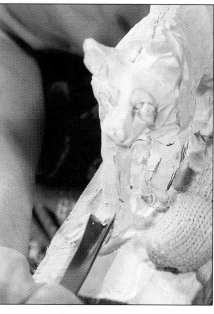

72 V-cut around the inside of the paw.

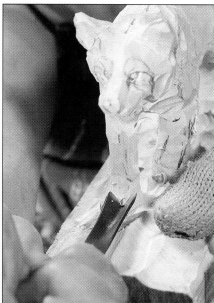

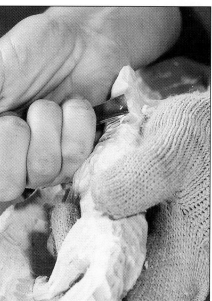

73 V-cut some texture on the neck area.

74 Stop cut between the toes.

75 Stop cut outside the toes.

76 Undercut the toes.

77 Shape up the piece.

78 Undercut the inside of the foot.

79 Trim up the back of the leg, making sure it tapers evenly down the leg.

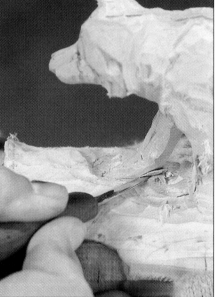

80 Cut the back of the wrist to the base with a carving knife.

81 Under-
cut the
last cut along
the base with a
carving knife.

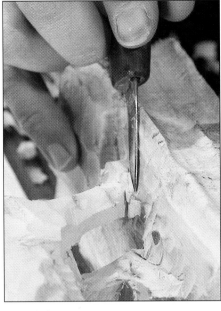

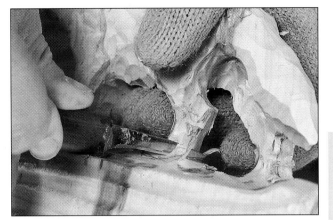

82 Cut the back of the leg, including the
Achilles heel, at an angle.

83 Texture the neck with a v-cut.

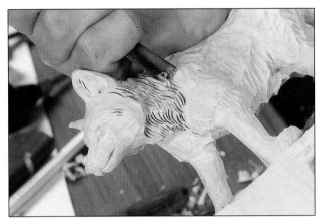

84 Continue texturing the body following the
hair tract chart.

Carving and Painting Do's and Dont's

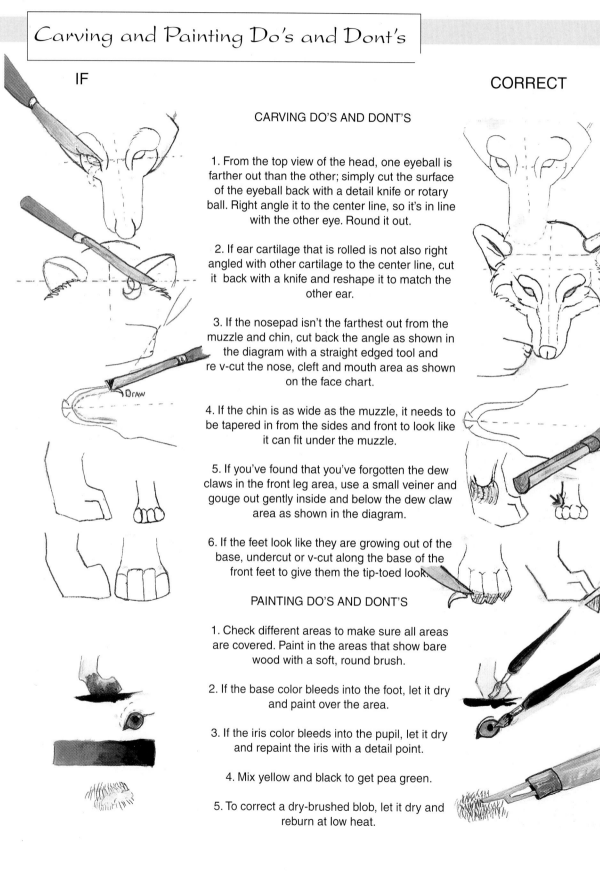

IF   CORRECT

CARVING DO'S AND DONT'S

1. From the top view of the head, one eyeball is farther out than the other; simply cut the surface of the eyeball back with a detail knife or rotary ball. Right angle it to the center line, so it's in line with the other eye. Round it out.

2. If ear cartilage that is rolled is not also right angled with other cartilage to the center line, cut it back with a knife and reshape it to match the other ear.

3. If the nosepad isn't the farthest out from the muzzle and chin, cut back the angle as shown in the diagram with a straight edged tool and re v-cut the nose, cleft and mouth area as shown on the face chart.

4. If the chin is as wide as the muzzle, it needs to be tapered in from the sides and front to look like it can fit under the muzzle.

5. If you've found that you've forgotten the dew claws in the front leg area, use a small veiner and gouge out gently inside and below the dew claw area as shown in the diagram.

6. If the feet look like they are growing out of the base, undercut or v-cut along the base of the front feet to give them the tip-toed look.

PAINTING DO'S AND DONT'S

1. Check different areas to make sure all areas are covered. Paint in the areas that show bare wood with a soft, round brush.

2. If the base color bleeds into the foot, let it dry and paint over the area.

3. If the iris color bleeds into the pupil, let it dry and repaint the iris with a detail point.

4. Mix yellow and black to get pea green.

5. To correct a dry-brushed blob, let it dry and reburn at low heat.

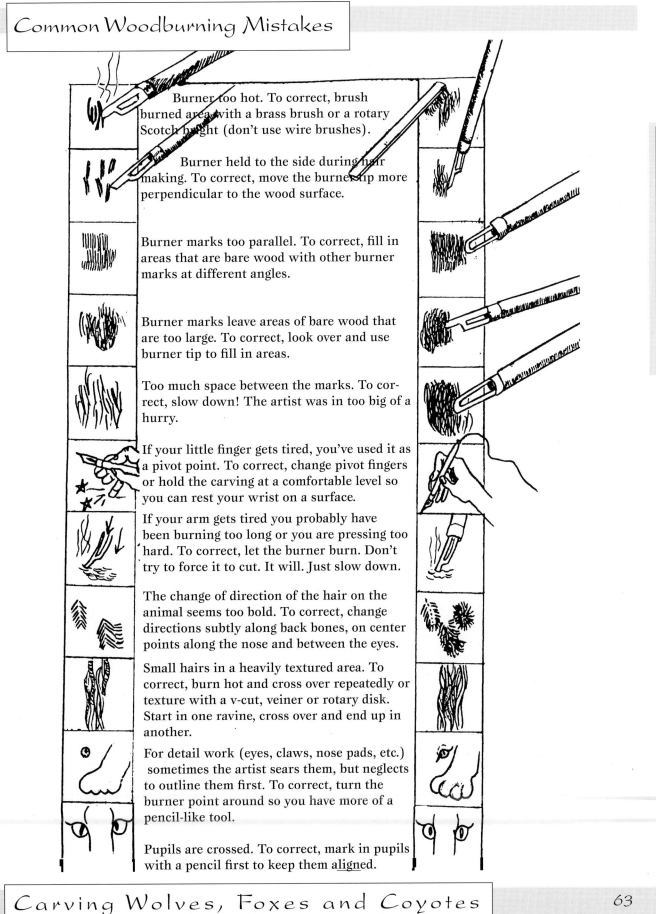

Burner too hot. To correct, brush burned area with a brass brush or a rotary Scotch bright (don't use wire brushes).

Burner held to the side during hair making. To correct, move the burner tip more perpendicular to the wood surface.

Burner marks too parallel. To correct, fill in areas that are bare wood with other burner marks at different angles.

Burner marks leave areas of bare wood that are too large. To correct, look over and use burner tip to fill in areas.

Too much space between the marks. To correct, slow down! The artist was in too big of a hurry.

If your little finger gets tired, you've used it as a pivot point. To correct, change pivot fingers or hold the carving at a comfortable level so you can rest your wrist on a surface.

If your arm gets tired you probably have been burning too long or you are pressing too hard. To correct, let the burner burn. Don't try to force it to cut. It will. Just slow down.

The change of direction of the hair on the animal seems too bold. To correct, change directions subtly along back bones, on center points along the nose and between the eyes.

Small hairs in a heavily textured area. To correct, burn hot and cross over repeatedly or texture with a v-cut, veiner or rotary disk. Start in one ravine, cross over and end up in another.

For detail work (eyes, claws, nose pads, etc.) sometimes the artist sears them, but neglects to outline them first. To correct, turn the burner point around so you have more of a pencil-like tool.

Pupils are crossed. To correct, mark in pupils with a pencil first to keep them aligned.

Woodburning a Wolf

Woodburning a Wolf

Recommended materials

Any woodburner with an adjustable thermostat will work fine. For the projects in this book, I've used a Detailmaster and tips 1A or 10A.

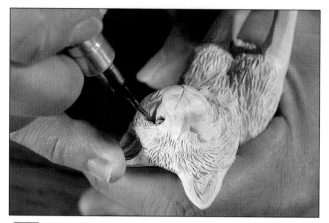

1 Put the burner tip (1A) into the inverted pyramid cut of the tearduct and pull it around the stop cut following the shape of the eye and leaning toward the eyeball.

3 Mark in the pupils with a pencil and push the point of the woodburner tip into the pupil. Gently move the tip from side to side.

2 This gives the illusion of the eyelid.

4 Put in the eyelid with the burner tip, pulling in the area of the socket.

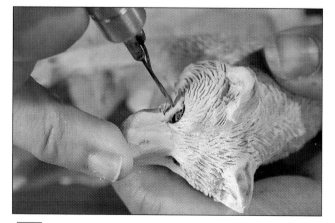

5 Use a stab-pull motion under the eye on the cheek.

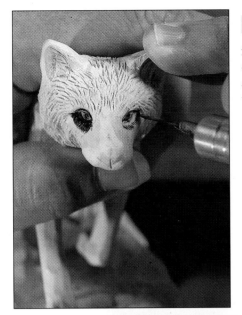

6 Use the illustration on page 30 as a guide for this area.

7 Pull longer strokes in the direction of the fur over the eye area (brow).

8 Use the illustration on page 30 as reference.

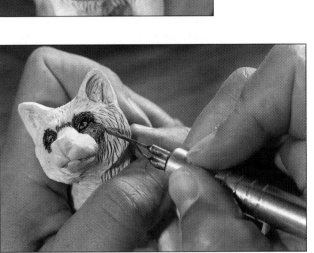

9 Use stab-pull method on the cheek area.

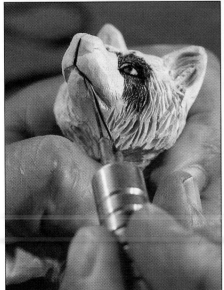

10 Place the woodburner point in the cleft of the nosepad area and follow the cut.

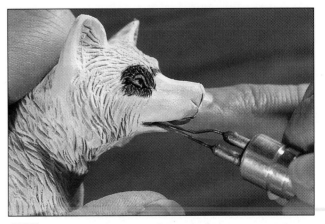

11 Cut down to the bottom of the muzzle. Continue to follow the cuts of the mouth toward the end of the mouth. Lean the tip downward to create the illusion of the end of the lip.

Carving Wolves, Foxes and Coyotes

12 For the nose pad, use the illustration on page 30 as a guide. First, burn the shape of the pad by leaning the tip onto the pad.

13 Pull the tip across, burnishing the nose pad to blacken it. Push in the point where you marked in the nostril.

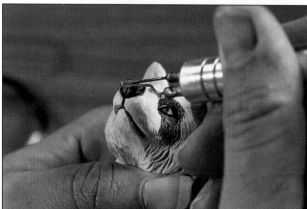

14 Gently push the point side to side until you get the hole of the nostril.

15 Cut the split of the nostril and pull to the outside of the pad.

16 With the point of the burner tip, mark in the dots where the whiskers are connected.

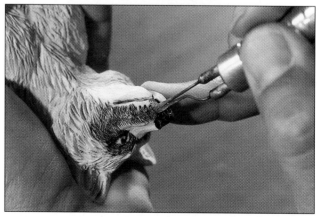

17 Start from the nose pad and stab-pull in a downward motion to show fur on the muzzle (see page 30).

18 After marking in the center point of the bridge of the nose, use the burner tip in a stab-pull motion. Gently change the direction of the fur along the center point (see page 30).

19 Change direction subtly under the chin.

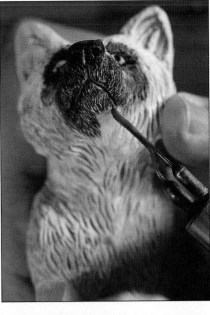

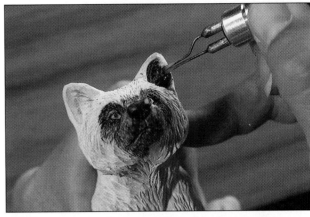

20 Pull the tip in the direction from the roll of cartilage of the ear inward to the hole of the ear. These burn marks give the illusion of guard hairs.

21 To give the illusion of a hole in the ear, press the point of the tip in and rock the burner back and forth.

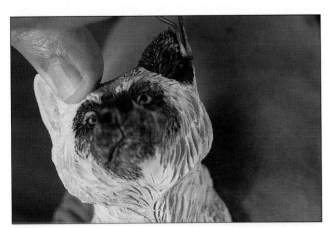

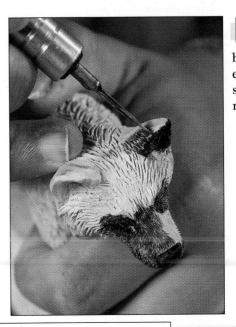

23 Burn the back of the ear, using a stab-pull motion.

22 Woodburn on the outside of the edge of the ear following the direction of the hair tract. This breaks up the surface of the cartilage giving the illusion of fur on the ears.

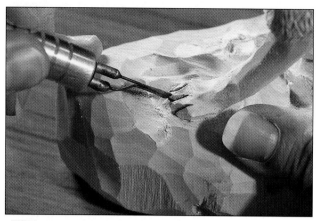

24 Push the burner between the toes to give the illusion of space between the toes.

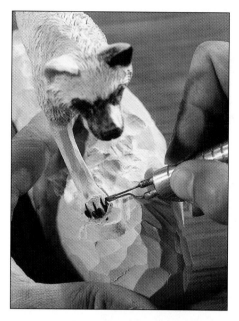

25 To achieve the illusion of claws, outline the claw shape and then burnish the claw.

26 Using the stab-pull method, burn in hair on each toe (see page 39).

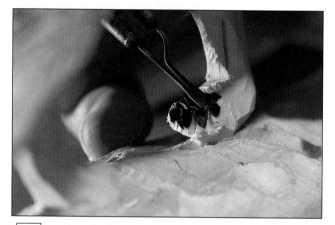

27 Sketch the bottom pads on the upturned foot. Place the burner tip along the edge of the pads, leaning the tip onto the pad. Pull the tip across inside the lines to burnish the wood.

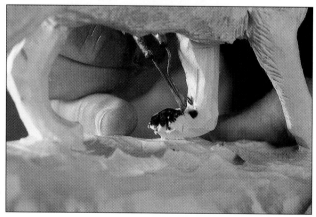

28 Stab, then pull the burner point in the direction of the hairs between the toes (between the pads).

29 The bottom of the upturned foot, when finished, will look like this. The pads have been burnished and hair has been burned between the pads.

Carving Wolves, Foxes and Coyotes

30 Changing the burner tip to 10A, pull the tip into the deep ravines of the textured areas.

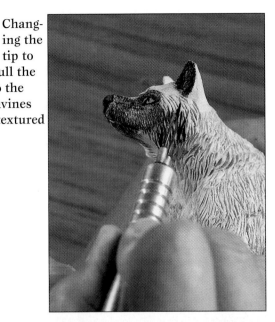

31 Cross from one ravine to another to break down the texture even more. Continue until you achieve the texture you desire.

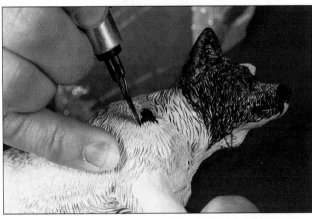

32 Continue burning the body of the wolf. This is a time-consuming process, and one that takes lots of concentration.

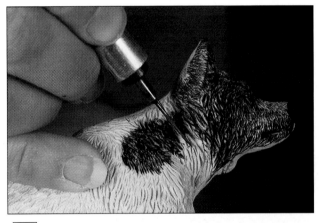

33 Remember, to make the burn marks look more like real hair, cross from one carved ravine to another. Keep going until you've burned the entire wolf. Now you're ready to paint.

Painting a Wolf

Painting a Wolf

Recommended materials

Brushes:
#00 detailer
#6 round
#8 flat bristle

Acrylic paints:
white
black
yellow ocra
raw sienna

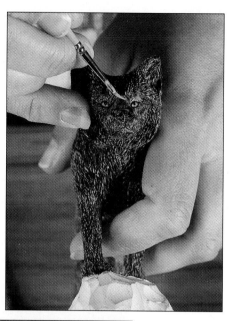

1 Using a #00 detailer or pointer, mix dull white acrylic paint with water until the paint reaches a milky consistency. Apply the white around the eyes.

2 Check the balance.

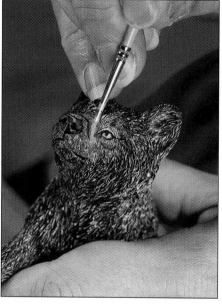

3 Paint along the sides of the muzzle, outlining the white areas.

5 Paint in the muzzle area.

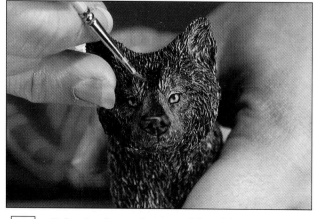

4 Paint in the eyebrows with white.

6 Paint white into the inside of the ears.

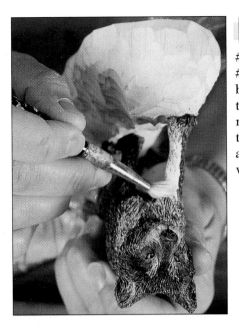

7 Using a large #6 round or a #10 flat brush, apply the white mixture to the white areas of the wolf's body.

8

9

10 With the #00 detailer (or pointer), apply the darker colors to the face areas. In this case it is a watered-down dark gray.

11 With the large #6 brush, paint the mixture over the other dark areas of the body.

Carving Wolves, Foxes and Coyotes

Painting a Wolf

12 With the #00 detailer, paint in the dark areas of the face, carefully placing the paint and keeping in mind that wolves are multi-colored.

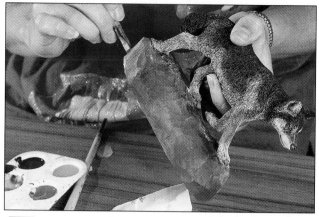

13 Mix the paint left on the palette and apply it to the base. Pay close attention to shadows.

14 Let the project dry while checking it over.

15 Using a #9 round or #8 flat stiff bristled brush, touch the brush tip to white paint and scrub lightly on the palette. Pull the paint in the opposite direction on the face.

16 Drybrush over the leg area.

17 Drybrush the shoulder.

18 Drybrush the legs.

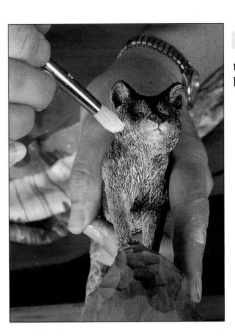

19 Drybrush the chest and belly area.

20 Continue drybrushing this area.

21 Drybrush the base and bottom area.

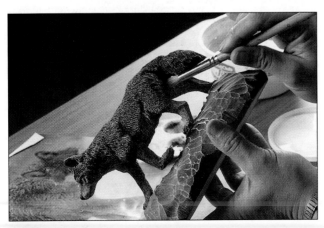

22 Continue drybrushing.

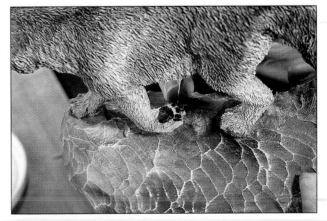

23 Again, using the #00 detailer, paint the pads on the bottom of the feet with black.

Carving Wolves, Foxes and Coyotes

24 Outline the mouth with black using a detailer.

25 Outline the eyelids with black.

26

27 Paint in the claws, including dew claw, with a detailer brush and black paint.

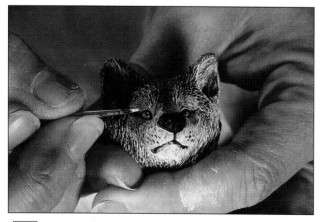

28 Put the finishing touches on the carving. A photo of the author's carving, titled *Lobo Lope,* appears on page 1.

Chapter Four
Patterns

Gray Wolf

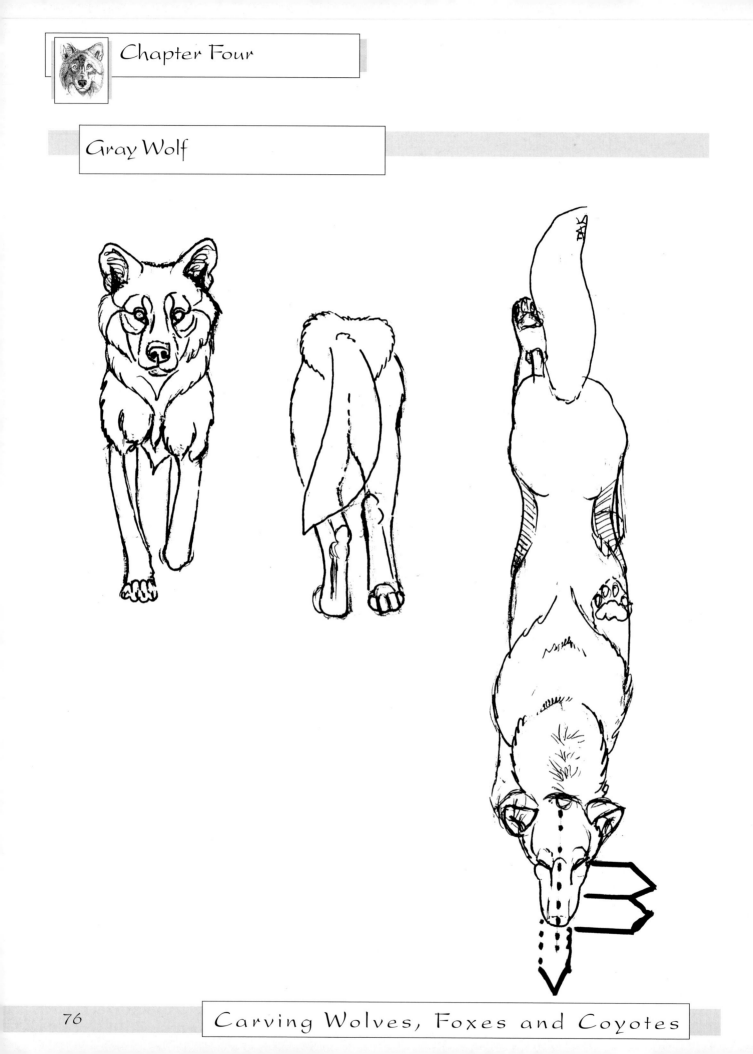

Gray Wolf

Sitting Coyote

Side

Top

Back

Red Fox

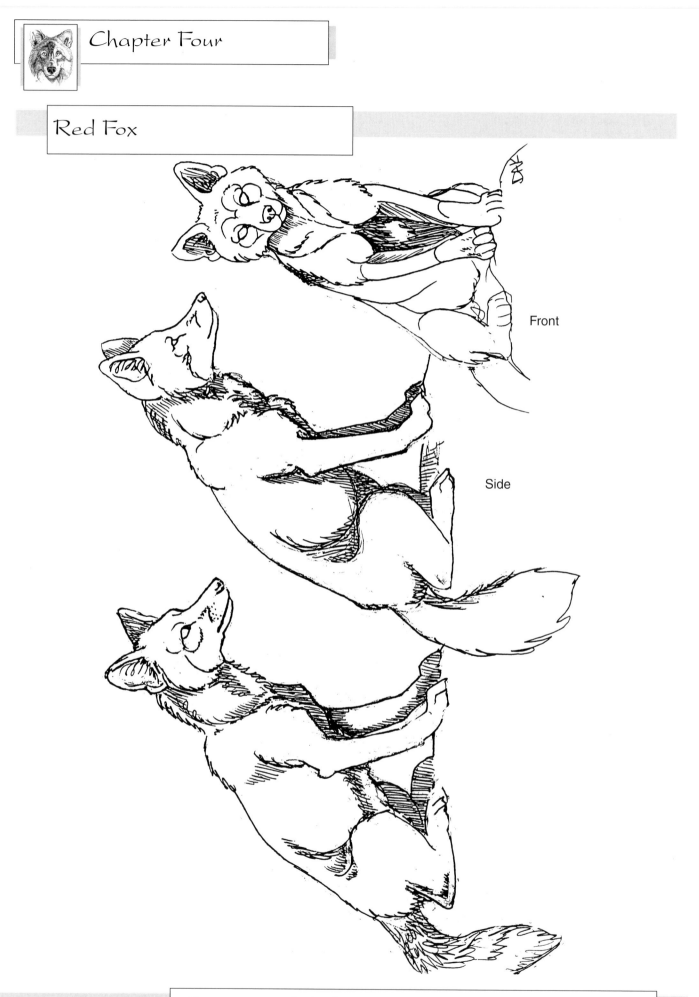

Front

Side

Carving Wolves, Foxes and Coyotes

Wolf in fox pose

Fox in wolf pose

Generic Pup Patterns

This pattern
was applied in
the fox piece

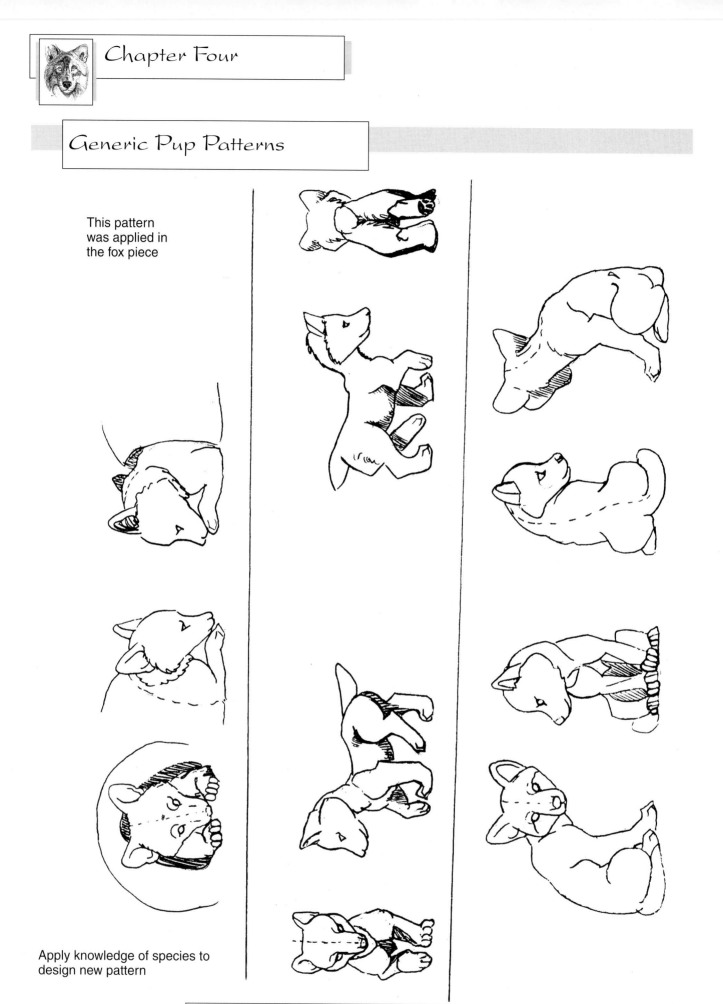

Apply knowledge of species to
design new pattern

Apply details of chosen species

Coyote
tail pose

With studies on sketches interchange the
heads and features with these patterns to
create new ones for groupings.

Puppy Poses

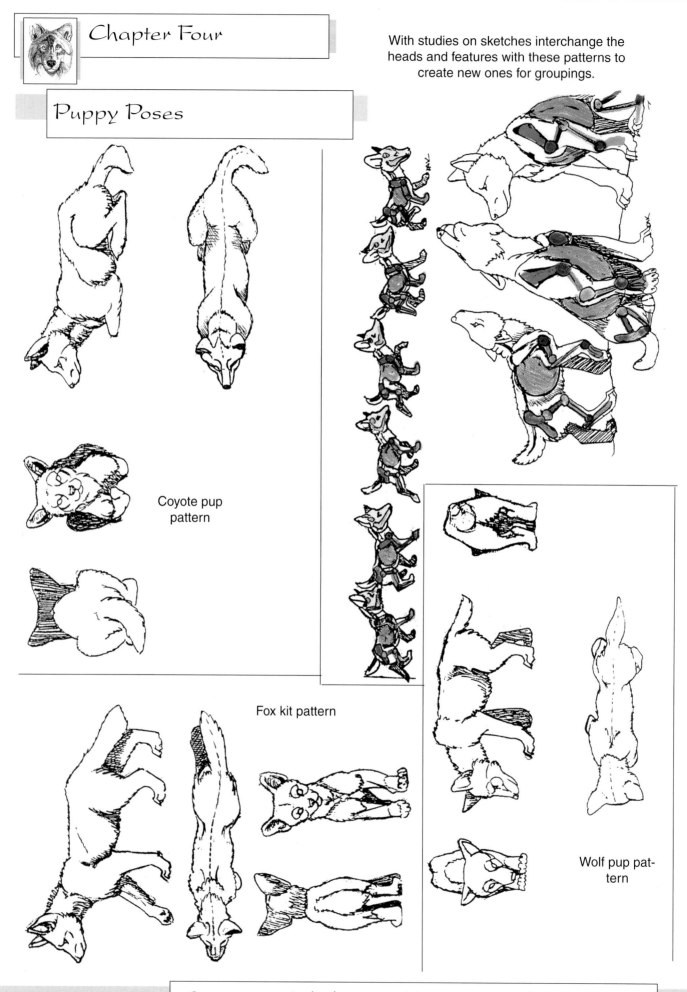

Coyote pup
pattern

Fox kit pattern

Wolf pup pat-
tern

Carving Wolves, Foxes and Coyotes

Appendix A: Illustrations

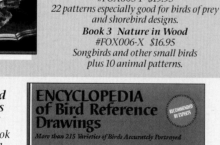

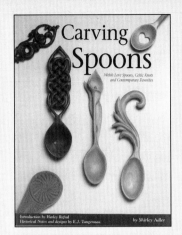

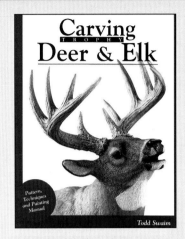

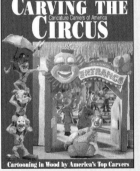

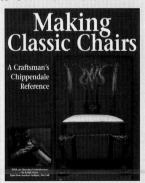

Animal Carving Books

Secrets from Desiree Hajny, Mary Duke Guldan and more!

Artistic Approach Books   by Desiree Hajny

Desiree is well known for teaching her students the "whys" of carving in addition to the "how-to." So you'll also learn about carving technique instructions. After you read one of these books, you'll be set to create a unique carvings reflecting your own personal style.

Carving Small Animals

Your source for rabbits, squirrels, and raccoons—North America's most popular small animals. Over 90 color photos show everything you need to know, with a special focus on hard to carve areas like eyes, ears, nose, and feet. Four complete patterns with accompanying anatomy charts.

#FOX073-6 $14.95

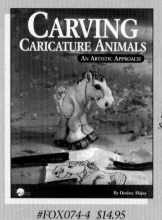

#FOX074-4 $14.95

Carving Caricature Animals

Desiree's caricature horses and mules are guaranteed to bring a smile to your face. Also included are otters, a junkyard dog, and more. Terrific section on caricature expressions for animals.

Big Cats
Carving Lions, Tigers and Jaguars

Learn to carve six different big cat projects inside. Over 90 color photos show you how step-by-step PLUS give valuable anatomy and reference material.

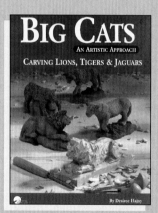

#FOX071-X $14.95

Mammals: An Artistic Approach

Playful otters, graceful deer and majestic bears are what you'll find in Desiree's first book. Sketches, photos, anatomy charts, carving and printing information are what you'll find inside this 168 page book. 18 patterns are also included.

#FOX036-1 $19.95

Mary Duke Guldan's Woodcarvers Workbook Series

"The best woodcarving patterns I have seen in my 40 years of carving." Ed Gallenstein, President National Woodcarver's Association.

For realistic, accurate, and easy to use patterns, these books simply cannot be beat! The secret is that each project is featured in every possible view—front, back, side, top and bottom—giving a 360° perspective of your piece. Best know for her animal patterns, her second book below also includes a wonderful pattern for a grandfather and grandson. We can't recommend this book highly enough. Terrific for all levels of carvers. Beginners will find these clear patterns helpful.

#FOX033-7 $14.95

Woodcarver's Workbook

14 patterns and step-by-step instructions for a wolf, moose, cougar, rabbit and wild mustang, unicorn, whitetail deer, dogs and a bighorn sheep.

See SPECIAL OFFER on Page D

Woodcarver's Workbook #2

No repeats from her first book. Instructions and patterns for Elk, Bison, Indian Chief, Horser, Human Figures, Oxen and more.

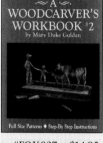

#FOX037-x $14.95

Complete Beginners Woodcarver's Workbook

Simply the best, easiest guide to carving ever! 10 projects illustrated in color with complete patterns and instructions. All you need is a knife and several simple gauges to get started.

Best Seller

#FOX085-X $9.95

Carving Wooden Critters
by Diane Ernst

A great collection of patterns, well drawn. 18 projects to make—playful puppies, sleepy otters, bunny rabbits and more. 4 views on each pattern.
#FOX038-8 $6.95

Best Seller

Carousel Horse Caving
by Ken Hughs

Back by popular demand. This is a classic of carousel carving how to, now updated and revised. Join Ken Hughs as he takes you step-by-step through carving a 1/3 size carousel horse. With your order, we'll ship you a fold-out cutting pattern.

#FOX072-8 $24.95

Easy ordering by phone
Credit Card orders please call 1-800-457-9112
Mail orders please send cover price plus $2.50 per book (maximum $5 shipping charge) to:
Fox Chapel Publishing Co., Inc. • 1970T Broad Street • East Petersburg, PA 17520   Page C

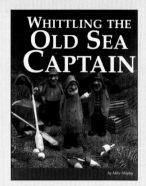
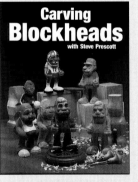
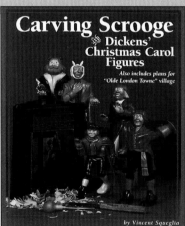
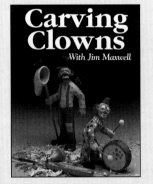
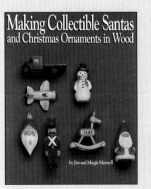
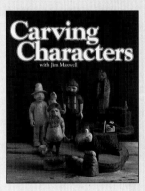

Hajny
Wood Carving
Studio

The best in woodcarving classes,

instruction, and reference material.

We offer classes by Desiree Hajny,

both here at our Colorado studio

or on-site at your location.

Patterns and videos by Desiree

available exclusively from us!

For more information please contact :